SELF-DEFENCE
for Women

SELF-DEFENCE
for Women

**Diana Warren-Holland · Denise Rossell-Jones
Rachel Stewart and *Women Against Rape***

HAMLYN

General Editor Rachel Stewart
Designer Glynis Edwards
Production Controller Richard Churchill

Published 1987 by Hamlyn Publishing
a division of
The Hamlyn Publishing Group Limited
Bridge House, London Road, Twickenham,
Middlesex, England

Produced by
Marshall Cavendish Books Limited
58 Old Compton Street
London W1V 5PA

© Marshall Cavendish Limited 1987

ISBN 0 600 50367 4

Typeset in Paladium by Quadraset Limited
Printed and bound in Italy

·CONTENTS·

Rape h Just how safe are we?

appeal in rap

How women can stand and fight sexual harassment

POLICE hunting th
men who raped
assaulted a wo
ing, west

Nightmare attack that wrecked a young mother's life

Three rape victims
who still live in fear

Council build
muggers haven

Battered wives
get little help
from police

HUGE RISE
IN RAPES

METROPOLITAN pol- prepar
report into domestic
lence, which
ve been co

ACTION AGAINST MALE VIOLENCE

Woman victim
of knifepoint
street attack

Who are
the
victims?

AN ARMED man held a young woman by the
throat at knifepoint in an
The 25-year

VIOLENCE AND WOMEN

BRUTAL SEX
ATTACKS ON
TWO GIRLS

Computer plan
to catch rapists

Yes, we can
fight back

already for
change in law
in rape cases

Martial
arts call
by nurses

500,000 nurses

A woman's silence can mean a rapist's freedom

on the crime statistics to try

8

·INTRODUCTION·
A MESSAGE FOR ALL WOMEN

ALL OVER THE WORLD, WOMEN ARE AWARE THAT MEN may attack them. We hope it is true that most men like and respect women, wanting to form good relationships as friends, relatives, lovers and husbands. But too many men obviously regard women as suitable targets for abuse, beating and sexual harassment, ranging from unwanted suggestions, fondling and groping, to rape and sadistic assaults.

Until recently, the only statistics available were those provided by the police, and it was not generally accepted that rape and sexual assault had reached epidemic proportions. It was mainly as a result of the survey carried out by Women Against Rape in London in 1985 that it was finally established that one-third of the female population is likely to be raped or assaulted in that city. These are the facts. Women are not being paranoid. We have genuine reasons for feeling afraid.

In our second chapter, Women Against Rape not only present the real facts, but they also argue strongly for the absolute right to defend ourselves and for the need for a safer environment, especially in terms of improved public transport and better street lighting.

If you yourself have been the unfortunate object of male violence, then you will find a wealth of comfort and advice in the first chapter of this book. You will also discover some reasons why many men resort to violence against women and what we can do to redress the balance in our society — firstly by learning about psychological self-defence. Through a positive, assertive mental approach, women will find that they can deal more easily with male aggression.

You may feel interested in learning some form of self-defence, not because you have suffered a physical attack, but simply because — like so many of us — you are determined to lead a full life, without the limitations imposed by fear. We all of us have the right to enjoy the freedom of the countryside, or the culture offered by cities, without feeling afraid. Physical self-defence skills will greatly increase your confidence and awareness and will open up innumerable fresh opportunities for you.

Because it is difficult to learn something new by yourself, it really is best to join a class and use the step-by-step techniques described in the third chapter for additional home practice and to increase your range of skills. If you feel ambitious enough to take up a martial art, then the last chapter will help you to choose one that is suitable.

All of the authors of this book are deeply concerned about women's safety. We do not seek violence and confrontations. We would all prefer kindness and friendship in a safer, more caring world. But we have individually experienced rape, assault or male harassment of some sort and have managed to find a way of working through these set-backs, either by helping and counselling others, by campaigning for increased safety or by learning and teaching self-defence and martial arts.

This book, therefore, is offered to all women in the hope that you will find something of value within these pages, and that through self-defence the quality of your life will be greatly enhanced.

PUBLISHER'S NOTE

The publishers wish to point out that, although every care has been taken in describing self-defence techniques, they cannot accept responsibility for any injury which might be incurred in carrying out the exercises. Any reader with doubts about her own health should first take medical advice.

Readers should find out about the laws on self-defence wherever they happen to live. This is particularly important regarding the use of force and the carrying or use of weapons. Under English law, it is at present illegal to carry weapons for self-defence purposes. British courts have generally allowed the use of force only if there is no other way to avoid an attack. Any force used must only be in proportion to the seriousness of the attack, and if possible you should escape or stop the attack without resorting to violence.

CHAPTER ONE

·COPING·WITH· ·MALE·VIOLENCE·

MOST WOMEN LIVE IN FEAR OF SOME KIND OF assault by men; they might be mugged and have their handbags snatched or their keys stolen. But far worse than this kind of attack, which is clearly motivated by theft, is the assault on their person. Rape is the ultimate terror in every woman's mind.

The psychological aspects of why some men choose to rape are important for women to understand. Although looking at these issues may be intellectually and emotionally traumatic, it may also help us to make clearer choices about how we can live in a society where we may feel we are in a state of siege, and where men may be seen as sexual terrorists. All women are potential victims, and age, looks, size and shape are irrelevant, therefore most of us are frightened. We may feel powerless. Because we have no way of knowing which men rape, we often find ourselves in danger. We perhaps want to trust men, but are unsure of their trustworthiness, and of how to cope if they are not. We need to be aware of what we can do if they rape or hurt us. This is a problem for many women because our upbringing results in many of us having a commitment to non-aggression. We do not like to hurt anyone, physically or emotionally.

We are not very good at saying what we want, and more especially what we do not want. Men do not seem to have this problem; they do seem, most of the time, to be able to say what they do and do not want. The problem for many of them is that they expect women to accommodate their wishes and not to deny or refuse them. This mismatch of internal and external realities experienced by men and women, creates a dilemma. Thus, men and women share a world, but have a very different view of it and of each other. How do we arrive at adulthood with such vastly differing views of such basic things? Or put another way, are rapists born, and are some women born to be victims of rape?

LEARNED BEHAVIOUR

Clearly men who rape are not destined from birth by some genetic factor to be rapists. They 'learn' attitudes and responses to women and to situations and become rapists. That this learned behaviour is an inappropriate response to the way in which they regard women, is indisputable. Most of us, certainly, wonder why some men want to hurt us and why they seem sometimes to hate us.

Women who are raped are not 'special' in the sense that they are genetically programmed to be rape victims. Primarily women and girls are raped because they are female. However, we are encouraged and praised as children, and later as women, for being passive, pretty and pleasing. It is these very qualities that may, from time to time, make life very unsafe for women. Being passive, pretty and pleasing does not easily co-exist with saying to a would-be assailant 'Go away.' For some of us, to retaliate using physical force would seem very difficult.

For all of us, both men and women, our behaviour is 'learned behaviour'; it is not genetically transmitted. This applies especially to the way in which we relate to other people and to our own personal attitudes and beliefs. Behaviour is acquired through a process called socialization. This is simply the method by which one generation transmits or passes on values, attitudes and ways of behaving to the next generation. Those involved in this ongoing process include parents, teachers, schools, the Church and the media. Thus, parents with a particular view of the world and of 'how we do things' and 'how we see people' and 'what we believe' will, probably unconsciously, choose friends, buy newspapers, select TV programmes, leisure activities and later, schools for their children, to reinforce and validate their belief system. Through this process children learn what is 'right' and 'good' and 'acceptable' in the eyes of their family.

Therefore, unlike genetic factors which cannot be permanently altered, such as eye colour and body height, by and large behaviour and attitudes are acquired or learned. Because what is learned can be unlearned it means we can, if we choose, relearn new, more appropriate ways of seeing ourselves and relating to one another.

In our society boy children are encouraged not to be cry-babies but to be brave and tough. They are praised for being competitive and winning is regarded as very important. Physical strength and being able and prepared, if necessary, to fight are seen as desirably masculine. Boys are not encouraged to show deep feelings of sadness and hurt, or even, past a certain age, of tenderness and love. These are regarded as sissy and later are overtly avoided by many men. Also boys are encouraged by both the family and society to develop confident, bold and aggressive traits. They are reared to be dominant and to expect deference, especially from subordinates and women.

Boy children who are well socialized in the western tradition grow up expecting power and an easy access to decision-making. Boys grow up internalizing the reality that they have privilege purely because of gender, because they are men. This is part of a very powerful ideology. In our hierarchical society men expect to be at the top of the pyramid with women underneath, both literally and metaphorically.

Women are seen as those who 'take care of their needs'. This includes cooking, washing, ironing, housework and child rearing. At work it involves ideally filing, typing, making the tea and generally massaging their egos. Thus men are left free to do the important things in life, earning money and gaining more authority, power and kudos. It also reinforces the early socialization experience that men 'do' things and women 'feel' things.

SOCIALIZATION OF MEN

Left: *At work, most men still consider that women should perform the more menial office duties such as filing and typing. Worse, some of them seem to think that any females are fair game for seduction. Many women are forced to leave their jobs as a result of this kind of harassment.*

GENTLE MEN

Men who have grown up in non-traditional families and who were not exposed to excessively sexist, conformist role models may have experienced problems with gender identity when young. They may have been mocked because they were not overtly aggressive, and their sensitivity and qualities of gentleness may have been described as unmasculine. However, men who have been socialized in this way are frequently able to relate very well to women.

This alternative process of teaching boys how to be men is very important in the whole debate about rape and sexual violence.

SEXUAL ATTITUDES AND BEHAVIOUR

Right: *Kerb crawlers are not necessarily dangerous, but they are always a nuisance. Many men are under the illusion that they have the right to leer at or chat up any woman on her own. They do not.*

'Real men always get their women.' And it is important, if you are a man, not just to get her but to bed her — or so men frequently believe. The more often a man does this the more he seems 'a real man' both to himself and to his peers. However, the truth is that many men find sexual situations both difficult and confusing. This is not unreasonable when their early socialization is taken into account. Toughness, not showing your feelings and expecting your own way, are not of themselves very useful skills for lovemaking. What is useful and desirable is for men to be able to speak of love and feelings and to be able to show softness, gentleness and patience.

Most women have been chatted up, touched up and some of us have been raped by men who appear to believe that women exist only for their use and benefit. False and dangerous though this attitude is it is extremely common. The notion that women enjoy and invite such behaviour is shared by many men across the social spectrum. The man on the building site yells 'Nice pair of tits love, give us a feel', and the managing director in the boardroom touches his secretary's breasts and murmurs 'You look very nice today my dear'. Both are exercising the commonly held male notion of 'If I like it I'll maybe touch it and if I like it a lot I'll have it'.

The kind of power inherent in this 'learned' masculine behaviour legitimizes for many men rape and sexual violence. This is not to suggest that all men rape. However, all men who are socialized within a patriarchal society learn that being a successful male means having and experiencing power. To be a powerless man in a western patriarchal society is to be an unsuccessful man. This thinking is especially located within the sexual arena.

FEELINGS AND COMMUNICATION

Men are very able to know and to say what they want, but they have considerable difficulty expressing what they feel. The process of male socialization does not encourage them to learn about feelings and communication through direct experience. In fact this is discouraged by casting doubt on the validity and worth of such behaviour. Consequently many men find it so hard to deal with their own feelings that they frequently do not want to experience them at all and block them off. This is not a useful exercise and is potentially disastrous when they are involved in relationships with women. Men often find it hard to cope when a woman cries and is sad. They tend to want to 'do' something whereas women would like them to 'feel' something, but this was probably not a way of behaving that they learnt as children, so the situation often makes them uneasy and uncomfortable.

Some men however are able both to experience their emotions and speak of them without feeling threatened or unmanly. As part of an interview, Paul recorded the following, 18 months after Sarah, his partner, had been raped:

'Well my feelings were extremely varied. The first thing was intense anger at the man. I was really angry deep inside and would undoubtedly have killed him if I'd managed to get hold of him. Although of course that would have gone completely against my professional training and my feeling for people. It was totally irrational. I found I was having to explain to myself what had happened and why it had happened. It just didn't seem conceivable that anyone could rape Sarah, but it *had* happened and I needed to put it into some order.

She can't lead the kind of life she lived before. It deprived her of a lot of freedom, which I resented — not only for Sarah, but in fact all women, because all women, one now recognizes, live under this same threat. I think unless it happens to you, you can't understand. And when it does, it's such a shock; a very deep traumatic shock.

Sexually, our relationship had ceased. I didn't feel rejected; but her reactions to noise, smell, the fact she couldn't be in the same room with men — as a psychologist I should have known. But I don't think the partner, however knowledgeable he is, quite understands the dynamics of the situation. It's something that is foreign to men. We don't easily understand, although we should.

Here was a woman who was emancipated, a feminist who had led a very full life; and suddenly it all stopped — he had no right to do that to her, no right at all.

What was also strange was the effect it had on me, sexually. It had got to the stage when I didn't have the sexual drives and desires that I had previously known. By this time I was beginning to resent other men as a sex — how on earth could one of my sex do this? And then, many months later, when we began to make love again — I began to see myself, even in the love situation, attempting to carry out an assault on the very woman I loved so much and whom I would *never* have subjected to such an indignity. I felt if I did make love to her I would almost be in the same role of the man who had hurt her so much.

I felt more love and protectiveness towards her than any sexual desire. I had a whole mishmash of ideas related to sex. So I had to go through a period of personal sexual and gender adjustment to the situation. I found it a very confusing time.'

REPORTING TO THE POLICE

If you have been raped and decide to report to the police:

☐ Find a friend or neighbour to support you

☐ Tell the police as soon as possible

☐ Do not wash or change: forensic evidence may be required

☐ Take fresh clothing with you

☐ Make notes of the events and any relevant details, to help you when making your statement

☐ Contact your local Rape Crisis Centre

☐ See your doctor (a police surgeon will not check for sexually transmitted diseases or pregnancy).

YOUR RIGHTS

When reporting sexual assault at the police station, if your country is governed by English law, you can:

☐ Ask to be questioned by a woman police officer

☐ Ask to be examined by a woman police surgeon

☐ Refuse to have your name read out in court.

THE RAPIST

All men can rape, but many choose not to. However, the man who rapes is exercising the considerable power that he enjoys within a patriarchal society. Rape is an extension of that male privilege of power. Rapists are not 'special' men; they are ordinary men who use their inherited power and capitalize on it, through rape.

According to Groth (1977) sexual desire is not the main reason why men rape. He cites the fact that rapists he has studied and helped all had access to sexual relationships, many of them very satisfying. In his research rapists were motivated more by anger and a need to experience power rather than for sexual gratification. He makes the point that men who rape are not all of one mind when it comes both to motivation and to attacking and hurting women. However, he has come to the conclusion that there are three components always present when a man rapes, which are anger, power and sexuality. The expression and variety of ways in which any of these components is shown, will vary from offender to offender. Groth makes three broad categories: the Anger Rape; the Power Rape; and the Sadistic Rape.

ANGER RAPE

This is to do with the man's need to lower the level of his feelings of extreme anger and rage. The rape is typified by the amount of aggression and degradation he inflicts on the woman. He uses more force than he needs merely to overcome her. Violence is of itself an important factor.

A life stress may be the trigger, which may be to do with a significant woman in his life — his girlfriend, wife or mother. Or he may have experienced some problems in other parts of his life. It could be a job loss or a physical fight. According to Groth the anger rapist does not report feeling sexual arousal at the time of the attack, but rather he feels troubled and hostile. Thus, using sex as a weapon to hurt and degrade, he sees the rape as an attempt to resolve and reduce his anger. Paradoxically, though, this kind of rapist may have erection problems during the attack. Satisfaction is gained anyway from the feelings associated with the discharge of anger, rather than the specific sexual release.

This kind of man has problems with the relationships he makes with women. They tend to be associated with a great deal of tension, explosive anger and irrational jealousy. He is frequently physically violent and hits them. According to Groth, the rapist in this category attacks and rapes women when his own relationships with women are in conflict.

POWER RAPE

In this type of rape the man only uses as much force as is needed to overpower his victim. This rapist wants complete control and power over the woman he attacks. He will use threats, both verbal and physical. He will try to make it impossible for the woman to refuse. He may have, or say he has, a weapon. The sense of control he achieves creates for him a renewed sense of power, strength and mastery. In this way he compensates for basic feelings of inadequacy, helplessness and vulnerability. In terms of personal relating skills, this kind of rapist is inept. He tends to feel worthless. He rapes in order to act out his fantasy of sexual and emotional control of women. Involved in the fantasy is the notion that the woman, although initially resisting, will succumb to his overtures and be impressed by his sexual performance. In reality this man may have sexual problems such as premature ejaculation and difficulty obtaining and maintaining an erection.

Groth's research shows that for this rapist the precipitating factor may be some form of behaviour or comment by a woman, which is interpreted by him as a 'put down' or a criticism. Rape in this context creates a setting in which the man may feel potent, masterful, strong and dominant. He is also able to suppress his real feelings of worthlessness, rejection, helplessness, inadequacy and vulnerability.

SADISTIC RAPE

In this category aggression itself becomes eroticized. The man enjoys sexually abusing the woman. He may severely injure her genitals, breasts and buttocks. He gains pleasure from her suffering, pain and distress. This kind of rape is primarily one of sadism. The man will plan the attack and it will be premeditated and calculated. He may even murder her. There may or may not be vaginal penetration, or he may use a bottle or other object.

According to Wyre (1986) rapists fantasize and plan their rapes well in advance. He believes that the process by which rapists masturbate to consistent images of rape and sexual violence is a problematic one. This research with rapists reveals that when a rapist masturbates to a fantasy of rape he is reinforcing his own distorted view of women and their place in society. In his fantasy the woman he thinks of and rapes may be someone important to him, whom he knows. In reality, when he acts out his fantasy and rapes, the woman he hurts so much is in a sense unimportant to him. Her significance is in terms of who she represents, rather than who she really is.

Women should be aware that a rapist does not choose to rape them because they look pretty or passive, but because they fit the key part in the rapist's scenario. He has selected a woman to play the part of the woman in his fantasy. In this situation the man acts out, via rape, some deeply complex attitudes and feelings about women. The raped woman is representative of a woman he wants to control and hurt. She is also part of a representation of a situation where he is, at least in fantasy, powerful and strong.

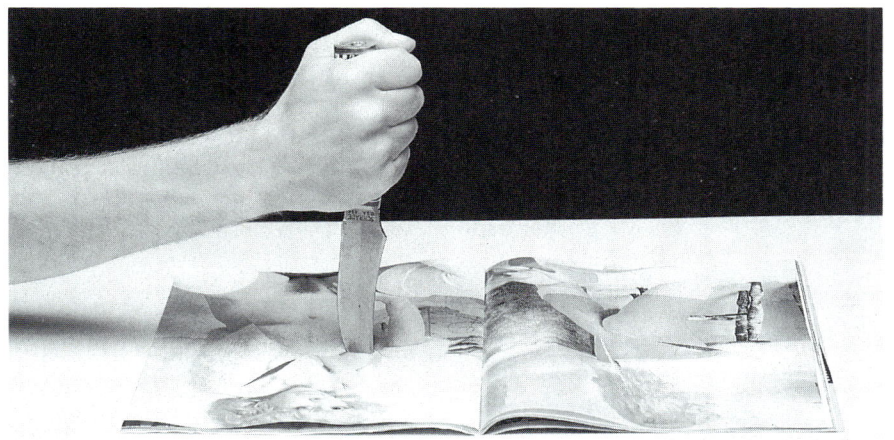

Left: *Many women are deeply concerned that 'girlie' magazines give men the impression that the opposite sex is perpetually available for seduction — or even rape.*

SOCIALIZATION OF WOMEN

Above: *Women in our society are encouraged to perform the domestic duties for men. All through their lives they are praised if they adapt easily to this subservient role.*

Women are socialized in a variety of ways, with the overall result of providing a fine service industry for men. The process does not equip us for an independent, self-determining life — nor is it intended to do. Within a patriarchal society primarily run by and for men, it is in male interest to produce women who are subservient, obedient and non-aggressive. Thus the powerful male dominant role is complemented. Girl children are encouraged and praised if they are gentle and loving. If they are pretty and act in a demure passive way they are rewarded with hugs, kisses and even presents. A lot of effort goes into the making of a socially acceptable woman.

Girls are not expected to argue, complain, raise their voices or to be rough. They are strongly discouraged from fighting and from developing any skills which may detract from the nurturing role ascribed to them by society. To fight is to be unfeminine. It is not seen as good or attractive; it is not rewarded. Praise is lavished upon girl children who are agreeable and compliant, and who later, as women, internalize the notion that men do know best and should be deferred to, especially where important decisions are concerned.

Learned helplessness and incompetence outside of the home are seen as attractive traits. These are positively encouraged. Competence within the home at cooking, housework and child rearing are regarded as low status, but vital to men, so paradoxically are presented as high status.

Young girls are encouraged to look sexy and attractive for men, but are also expected to be 'good', and the responsibility for male desire and sexual behaviour is placed with them. Indeed, women are praised for being sexually ambiguous. Media representations of female desirability are recreated daily, especially through advertising. However, we are only expected to *look* sexual and not to *be* sexual. If we do celebrate and enjoy our sexuality in a way that pleases us; if we do ask more sexually from men than they wish or are able to give; if we commit the ultimate sin of highlighting their sexual shortcomings and failures, we are criticized and regarded as sluts. This in turn creates guilt and confusion about our bodies and about our sexuality.

THE DILEMMA OF FEMININITY

If a woman has been successfully socialized in western terms, she will experience some ambivalence about competing in the world with men on their terms, and she will tend to see herself in this role as unfeminine and undesirable. Many women resolve this dilemma by combining low-status work outside of the home with child-rearing and home-making. Women who achieve academically and who reject the role of nurturer and home-maker in order to fulfil their own ambitions, are often regarded by men as unnatural, pushy and aggressive. In advertising, such women are rarely role models.

One of the tragic results of traditional female socialization is that we tend to be excessively, inappropriately polite and nice. Many women have admitted that when they were attacked they were not able to say 'Don't do that' or 'Go away', but said instead 'Please don't hurt me'. This culturally induced passivity is not useful or productive for women. We are strong. We need to reclaim and learn to use that strength. We need to feel that it is good and right. We should *never* feel that such behaviour is unwomanly.

The notion that abounds in our culture that only 'certain' women are raped is a false and dangerous one. This view suggests that if you are raped it must have been your own fault and that you must have done something to provoke the man to rape you. This places the responsibility for the fact that men rape, with women. It is this argument that, taken to its logical conclusion in the courts, allows rapists to go free. The argument therefore goes that if you do not wear 'tarty' or provocative clothes, go out late at night, or look sexy and attractive, you will be safe. The reality is quite different. You may be safe, or you may not be. It really has very little to do with clothes, make-up, hair style, or where you have been or where you are going. It is not a moral issue, although for women who have been raped it may be clear that at least some of society sees it that way.

Women who are raped and who, in the eyes of society, obviously break the rules, will be very firmly told that they are to blame. This will include women who hitch-hike, women who go out alone at night, lesbian women and prostitutes. They will be held up to the rest of us to show what happens if we do not do as we are told. The print media are especially active in the promotion of this view. Women who keep the rules and yet still are raped may wonder who moved the goal posts! This is also useful for the media; it allows them to present such women as 'good and pure'. It may also be used to serve as a warning: if 'good women' are raped, what more can happen to a 'bad woman'?

The reality of course is that women do not cause men to rape. Our clothes, our sexual orientation and our life styles are irrelevant. We are raped because we are women and because we fit the part at that moment in the rapist's piece of action. No more. No less. For this we cannot be held individually or collectively responsible. The powerful mythology that surrounds the issue of sexual violence, and places the responsibility for rape with women, is one that should be put into perspective:

WHO GETS RAPED AND WHY?

DISPELLING THE MYTHS

Don't go out without clothes — that encourages some men.
Don't go out with clothes — any clothes encourage some men.
Don't go out alone at night — that encourages men.
Don't go out alone at any time — any situation encourages some men.
Don't go out alone with a female friend — some men are encouraged by numbers.
Don't go out with a male friend — some male friends are capable of rape.
Don't stay at home — intruders and relatives can both rape.
Avoid childhood — some rapists are 'turned on' by little girls.
Avoid old age — some rapists 'prefer' aged women.
Don't have a father, grandfather, uncle or brother — these are the relatives who most often rape young women.
Don't have neighbours — these often rape women.
Don't marry — rape is legal within marriage.
To be quite sure — don't exist.

This is, of course, another way to look at it.

HOW SHOULD WOMEN BEHAVE?

All women must decide for themselves how to live to feel as safe and strong as is possible in a society where there is so much male violence. Many women may argue that it is for men to change their aggressive behaviour patterns, and others will say that women should not add their own violence to that of men. Both of these arguments have some validity, but most of us need to know how to cope now; men have yet to change and many women say that they will not be raped or abused again. So how should we behave? What can we do to feel safe? An American study (*Stopping Rape*, 1985) found that the most effective way to prevent rape is to scream and yell and to use physical force. In terms of the legality of carrying weapons, in Britain the only legal weapon is a shriek alarm (screechy whistle). Many women do carry items that they think they would use if attacked. These include perfume, hairspray, combs, pepper and some women risk carrying knives. The law says that if you carry any object for the express purpose of self-defence you may be charged with carrying an offensive weapon. We all have to decide for ourselves what the right action is.

In a sense, making this decision and talking and thinking through the issues involved is a personal commitment to saying 'I will not be put down', 'I will not be raped'. We should be aware that most of us need to re-learn the ways in which we behave in order to keep ourselves safe. We should try and regard this experience as one of growth and learning, to be proud of it — even our small successes. It will probably be useful to talk to women friends and share experiences. Getting some feedback may provide validation and is a helpful tool for learning. This whole exercise can be very positive and a source of strength, especially if we are unsure.

HOW TO HANDLE A POTENTIALLY VIOLENT OR DANGEROUS SITUATION

On the whole women tend to react instinctively. Usually that reaction is linked to how we see ourselves in the first place. Women who have a poor self-image and lack assertiveness are not likely to protest, scream, run or physically fight back. Women who are assertive and have a good self-image may well be able to do all of those things and more. And then again, they may not be able to. It is very important that women are not made to feel guilty because they have been in a situation where they were unable to fight back, either psychologically or physically. The aim, if you find yourself in a difficult or potentially violent situation, is to stay safe and if possible feel good about the way in which you reacted. It is important to feel that you did all you could at the time. If you judge the situation to be unsafe, then trust your feelings and do not wait around to see if it worsens. Get out! If you are able to go, then do so, decisively and with speed. If it is a false alarm don't be embarrassed. If you do upset a man — so what? It is better to be alive and seen as aggressive/unfeminine, than hurt or dead but very polite. Be aware of danger and look for potential hazards in situations. Learn to trust your own feelings. If you feel uneasy about a situation trust that feeling and *do not stay*.

If you realize too late that the situation is potentially violent and you cannot get away, try not to look or feel intimidated. Be calm and aware. Make eye contact and gaze steadily. It is useful, but not always possible, to try and create an internal sense of outrage: 'How dare this man say this/do this to me?' or 'How dare he make me feel unsafe?' This will help you to feel and transmit a sense of anger and hostility, and locate the responsibility for his wrong doing with *him*. If you are going to use self-defence, be mentally alert and ready and get in early. Apologize later if you are wrong! Remember that even if the man is known to you, in terms of sexual violence he is probably an unknown quantity: he could operate in a variety of ways. So plan on staying alive and not being raped or abused in any way. Learning to judge a situation and then trusting that judgment enough to act on it can be a liberating experience. So no self blame. We all do what we can in situations.

One of the most important factors to be aware of is that there is no 'right' way to react to the crime of rape or sexual violence. Each of us will react in an individual way, to what may have been a life-threatening situation. That way is valid and right for each of us; it is what we need to do, or how we need to feel, and it should not be challenged or criticized.

When we are raped, although our bodies may be hurt and invaded, our minds suffer the most. We may feel that we have lost our dignity, our self-esteem and our self-determination. The event may colour all aspects of our lives. This is especially likely in the psychological sense, either for a short or a long term. Women may experience an ongoing sense of being 'overpowered' and 'out of control' in terms of day-to-day living. Since most women are socialized into the role of 'carer', they may feel pressurized by the expectations of family and friends to 'get over' being raped fairly quickly and return to normal 'caring' duties. This is a time when women need to be cared for. It may last for a long time. However long or short, the woman is not trying to get attention or deliberately being difficult and unreasonable. Women do not 'get over' rape and sexual violence in the same way, and with the same speed, that as children they got over chicken-pox.

There are many emotional reactions to deal with and they will probably vary in intensity from day to day, depending upon the woman, her psychological reserves and the responses of those around her. However, the main reactions of women are to feel ashamed and guilty. Most experience a sense of stigma or 'differentness', which they feel other people are able to see. The initial reaction is to wash and bath, almost ritualistically, because the raped woman feels dirty and worthless. Her confidence and sense of self-esteem vanish. So too does her sense of being sexually autonomous. She may not want to have any sexual contact, even with someone she loves deeply.

Our sexuality is central to our sense of being, so when we are raped we experience a great sense of personal loss. This 'loss of self' can be a very frightening and disorientating experience for a woman. The more so, if the woman previously was confident, had a good self-esteem and a satisfying sexual relationship. Suddenly, almost within minutes, this has all disappeared and she is confronted with a stranger — herself, but someone that she does not know.

It is small wonder that at this point many women turn to alcohol or tranquillizers to dull the pain and confusion that they are experiencing. In fact, it is at this point that the woman enters a 'bereavement' state. The loss is her selfhood. But amidst all the turmoil it may be difficult for

HOW WOMEN REACT TO RAPE

Above: *It may be a long time before a woman who has suffered serious sexual assault feels able to take control of her life again.*

her to understand, in any meaningful sense, the bereaving of 'herself'. Also it is confusing, because if she is bereaving the loss of 'herself', then who is she? This grieving process is very painful, but is an important component of general healing and recovery following rape and sexual violence. It is important, however painful, and however long it takes, that the woman is given time and space to mourn her loss, the bereavement of her essential self. It is only through experiencing this bereavement and eventually accepting this loss that the woman will be able to become and feel whole again.

Listed are some of the commonly experienced reactions to having been raped or sexually abused. However, it must be stressed that *all* responses are 'right' and 'normal', in whatever proportion and at whatever time they occur; they are part of the process of recovery and reintegration. It is hoped that this will reassure women who have been raped, and who perhaps fear that they are going mad.

SHOCK

The initial reaction to rape is severe shock. This may be manifested in a variety of ways. Some women are hysterical and tearful while others may be very calm and still. Many women are silent and withdrawn. Other women act outwardly in a very cool rational fashion; some describe a sense of numbness and disbelief. Other women describe the rape and post-rape experience as having a dream-like quality and of expecting to wake up, as from a nightmare. Yet others refuse to accept that anything has happened to them.

It is always very important to believe what a woman says. If you know someone who has been raped, do not base your reactions on her reactions. Remember that she is in shock, and people in shock do not always behave, in that situation, as we would expect.

Right: *Tears can be a means of releasing the complicated emotions that result from sexual assault or rape.*

FEAR

Some women react to intense fear with great anger, and scream and yell and physically retaliate. Other women, sensing danger and being fearful, run away. These two reactions illustrate simply what is called the Fight or Flight reaction. Our bodies and minds are geared to respond in one of these ways when we find ourselves in danger.

However, in western society women are socialized into more gentle ways. We are taught not to fight, but that it is right and good to be passive. This learned behaviour that is superimposed on our biological heritage is not useful to us in a society where some men want to rape and hurt us. Thus, very many women faced with a violent situation will not have been able to respond to attack with the flight or fight reaction, but rather will have physically and psychologically 'frozen'. They are terrified of being killed. They are unable to scream or yell or fight back.

The debilitating effects on a woman who has responded to fear by freezing may be long-lasting, and she may carry on being fearful long after having been raped. In this situation the actual feeling of fear and of all the emotions and limitations it produces, is an extremely negative experience for the woman. Women who are not able to fight back physically or psychologically may experience a sense of guilt. They may also find it difficult thereafter to confront and deal effectively with other life stresses.

ANGER

Not all women who have been raped immediately feel anger. Those who do, describe it as a mixture of fury towards the man who raped them, contempt for a society that is so casual and uncaring about the women who are hurt and raped by men, and annoyance with themselves for not preventing it. However, it is a problem for women in western culture to experience anger. Because as children we are not taught to express and to feel our anger, it is usually something we have to learn to do, generally as adults. Women who have not learned to cope with their anger and express it have particular difficulties when they are raped.

In this situation women frequently displace the anger and blame themselves, instead of the man who raped them. Women have the absolute right to be very angry if they are raped. Placing the blame and responsibility for the rape with the man, will help to create a situation where the constructive anger necessary for healing and growth, can be felt and experienced.

GUILT

Women who have been raped frequently experience feelings of guilt. Because women are taught to feel responsible for almost everything in life, and especially for men's sexuality, to feel guilty about being raped is an extension of that thinking. In a society where rape jokes abound and where women are portrayed as sinner or saint, it is almost inevitable that the raped woman will feel she was, in some way, to blame. Thus, women are plagued by doubt: 'What did I do/not do?' 'Did I cause, or want it to happen?' 'Was it the way I was dressed?' 'Why didn't I scream, fight or run?' And of course the most problematic question for raped women is 'Why me?' Since society supports the curious notion that women are to blame when men rape, and this thinking is reinforced through the media, it is most likely that women will experience some guilt.

NIGHTMARES

Many women have nightmares after being raped. They often find it difficult to fall asleep because they are frightened of dreaming and because they are very tense and anxious. Having nightmares and reliving through dreams the trauma and pain of rape are debilitating and lonely experiences. The dreams and nightmares happen at the precise time that the woman needs sleep. During periods of stress, sleep is a very important way of building up energies and renewing emotional strength. Many women experience nightmares night after night and become very tired, depressed and even more stressed.

Often women find that through talking about the nightmares, and about the actual rape, they are able gradually to work through the experience. The nightmares may last for a long time, but they will go eventually. They usually lessen as the woman shares with someone else her hurt and fear of showing anger. Many women find it useful to go to sleep with the light on. It is also reassuring to be able to be with someone during this time, or at least be able to phone a parent, lover or friend for support.

LOSS OF SEXUAL FEELINGS

Ideally when we make physical love with a partner we also involve our minds and feelings. Thus, lovemaking is a reciprocal act of the giving and taking of pleasure, both mentally and physically. Rape is a very violent and direct abuse of our bodies and minds. So one of the first reactions to being raped is to lose interest in sexual lovemaking.

Some women are unable to have any physical contact with any man. Others say that they just wanted their partner to cuddle them and hold them. The loss of sexual feeling, even with someone she loves deeply, can be a very confusing experience for the woman. If she has previously been able to enjoy her own sexuality and to enjoy sexual loving, to lose this capacity, or even to dislike the thought of it, may be a disturbing experience. In a loving sexual situation a woman may safely and joyfully experience both her own strength and her own vulnerability; when she has been raped it is likely that she will regard her own sexuality with disinterest or even distaste.

Many women are fearful of sex after rape. It is important that the woman should feel 'in charge' of both her own body and of the sexual situation, in any relationship she may have. Some women fear that they have lost the capacity to express physical love. This is probably not true, but frequently women do not want to make physical love for a long time. There is no set 'normal' time scale for this. Certainly women should never allow themselves to be pressured into 'let's just try'. This will only result in her feeling even more powerless and out of control.

Sexual feelings usually return as the woman gains control once more of other areas of her life.

CHANGE IN BODY IMAGE

Women often speak of 'disowning' their body following rape or sexual assault. They feel a general sense of dirtiness and unworthiness. Paradoxically, at the same time as disowning their body, many women keep on taking baths and showers, as though ritualistically trying to wash away the experience. Women may find that at this time they actually dislike or even hate their body. It becomes a focus for all the sadness, pain and anguish that they are experiencing. Many women change the way they dress and want to appear ordinary and unnoticed.

Left: *Some women may wash themselves compulsively after rape, in an effort to feel clean again.*

If you have been raped, do not tell yourself it just did not happen — that you imagined it or dreamt it. Try not to isolate the experience in your mind. We all want, at some time, to do that, but it is not productive or useful. Being raped is truly awful. By acknowledging it as a part of your life and experience you are, in a sense, taking back the power that the rapist seized. Refuse to be psychologically tied by him. Confront the pains and the fears. As you confront them, so very gradually they will lessen and go. It is good of course to do all this with the support of someone who loves you and cares about you, especially if they go on loving you and caring when you get it wrong or over-react. Women friends, too, may be a source of love and support. Talking with other women, especially women who have been raped, will help. Always remember — you were not to blame, it was not your fault.

PSYCHOLOGICAL SELF-DEFENCE

Self-defence is primarily about using body moves and tactics. Psychological self-defence, first and foremost, is to do with 'mind moves' and behaviour. Just as with physical self-defence new ways and techniques have to be learned, so it is with psychological self-defence. Both are about keeping safe and feeling good about yourself.

Underpinning psychological self-defence is the notion that you have both the right to make choices, and the right to control your own life and to be self-determining. These are attractive possibilities for women, but they are also challenging and potentially risky ones. We are not taught to please ourselves, so we have to learn. As with learning any other new skill it can be exciting and rewarding, but first you have to believe that you have the *right* to learn and use the skill!

BEING IN CHARGE

It is important to respect and trust your right and your ability to make choices and to act on them. Even to do nothing is a choice, and sometimes this may be sensible; it may even save your life. The crucial factor is that you should be in charge of your own life.

Try to validate your own experiences, and do not minimize them by acting as though what has occurred is unimportant to you. For example:

> 'Well he only hit me in the face and took my car keys. It could have been much worse. I could have lost some teeth and he could have taken the car!'

Regard such an attack as this as a very serious one indeed. It is better not to compare it with a friend's experience, especially if she lost her car and all her front teeth! If you do, you are likely to think that by comparison what was done to you was tiny and unimportant.

To take control of your life means, for many women, learning new ways of behaving and of relating to other people. Implicit in this is learning to say what you want and what you do not want. It does not mean you will, or should, always have your own way, but that you are clear about what you would like. This creates the possibility for both negotiation and if necessary compromise. Making choices means also taking responsibility for the outcome of those choices.

Being very fearful, and feeling unable to cope with that fear, hinders women and prevents them from being fully adult self-determining people. It is important to learn to accept and understand fear. By doing this it becomes controllable. Being fearful does not of itself mean that you are weak, but rather that you are valuable and worth taking care of. Strong women feel fearful. It is a crucial and necessary reaction to dangerous situations.

Have you ever said or thought, 'I felt there was something peculiar about him, but told myself not to be stupid'? Discounting yourself in this way can put you in danger. It is most important to rely on our own intuitive feelings about fear, to trust them and to be strong enough to act on them.

ASSERTIVENESS

Assertiveness is the key to psychological self-defence. Being assertive is not the same as being aggressive. Assertiveness means being direct and saying what you mean without making excuses, apologizing, or justifying your rights in the matter. In order to be able to learn the techniques of assertiveness, it is necessary to develop self-confidence. A lot of women have problems about being self-confident and, for example, find it nerve-racking to speak out in groups or at their place of work. This is especially so if these are male-dominated situations. However, it is important to learn the lessons of assertiveness, in order to develop and use your own psychological self-defence. Assertiveness is positive

Left: *Assertiveness and a positive, confident outlook will affect your whole life, not just at work, but in your ability to enjoy yourself, especially when you are on your own.*

behaviour. Women are often confused because the messages that they want to convey are frequently misunderstood, or misinterpreted. By living assertively there is no risk of sending double messages or being misunderstood. To be assertive is to be strong, in control and to exercise choice: this makes psychological self-defence possible. It is also an affirmation of the fact that you do matter, and what you want or feel in any given situation should not, arbitrarily, be dismissed.

By not being assertive, but by being 'well-socialized', women inadvertently reinforce the male view that they do not mind being leered at, touched, groped or raped. Also that they do not mind being spoken of, not as complete women, but as 'parts'. For example: 'Nice arse on that one'; 'What great knockers', and so on. Women do mind. Most find this kind of behaviour degrading and insulting, and they are not generally flattered. The process of 'taking women to pieces', albeit verbally, is a psychologically damaging experience for women in terms of their self-perception. It can also cause them to feel powerless and out of control. If, because of male comment, you perceive yourself basically as 'the one with a good arse', it is very difficult to feel and to be a strong self-determining woman and to be assertive.

So what can women do? One way is to make it quite clear to men that you do not want to be spoken of in this way, that you do not find it flattering, amusing or pleasant. A frequent male response to a woman behaving in this assertive way, is to be told: 'You'll be sorry when it stops' or 'Frigid bitch'. Women find it very hard to cope with this well-learned and practised male behaviour and they are often annoyed by their own feeble responses. However, by learning to be assertive and by using psychological self-defence, the dynamics of the situation can be changed. It is certainly not possible always to alter the situation, but different responses and ways of handling those situations can be learned. If you feel confident about saying what you want, it is likely that you will be able to say to unwanted male attention: 'Take your hands off me'; 'No, I don't want to go inside/outside/into the bedroom'.

Body language too, changes when you are being assertive. If you feel confident and sure of your rights, your body movements and speech will mirror this fact. This is very important as a way of life, not just useful if you are returning a pair of faulty shoes.

A good way to start practising this is when you walk through groups or crowds and when you enter a room.

Many women think of assertiveness as being useful only when warding off a possible attacker. However, there are very good reasons why it is a useful skill for women in our culture in terms of daily life. Because women are socialized into roles that 'put others first', it is often assumed that they do not know what they want. The majority of women do know very well what they want. The difficulty for many women is that to say so, unequivocally, would appear unfeminine and aggressive! Women suffer psychologically from such restrictions, by feeling resentful, powerless and unimportant. This loss of control and power-lessness can be changed by women daring to be assertive. Basically you learn it by doing it! Our own attitudes about ourselves are of importance throughout this whole process.

People do not look after the things they regard as valueless and of no worth. It is good to see our minds and bodies as unique and precious, to take great care of them in order to ensure that no one damages or invades them. To this end, learning self-defence can be very useful in acquiring the skills of assertiveness which underlie psychological self-defence. The process of learning self-defence puts women in touch with their own bodies. This is a valuable experience, breaking down barriers and fears about what the female body is able to do. Women frequently report a realization of their own strength and their physical and psychological potential when they have been involved in self-defence.

Clearly physical self-defence has strong links with psychological self-defence, especially with regard to fear. Many of us are scared of saying and doing the wrong thing and, at a physical level, of getting hurt. We need to trust our psychological strength and to experience our physical ability.

If you feel silly and self-conscious practising alone, get together with friends and learn in a group. Self-assertive skills will help you to feel stronger and more conscious of yourself as a valuable, worthwhile person. They should also help you to feel less of an 'object' to be used and consumed.

These are not easy lessons for women, especially when they have a lifetime of learned 'ladylike' behaviour behind them. However, they are within every woman's reach; it is for each of us to decide what to do, and how we are going to live the rest of our lives.

PRACTISE

☐ Walking tall

☐ Looking and feeling confident about yourself

☐ Speaking clearly and firmly

☐ Eye contact — meeting and holding a gaze.

LEARN

☐ To scream and yell

☐ To say and shout 'No' and 'Go Away'.

HOW TO START LIVING AGAIN

Listed are some positive suggestions for approaching life during the extremely difficult and traumatic adjustment period after rape or sexual assault. Women should also rely on their own judgments and feelings about how they can best cope.

Give yourself time and emotional space. If you had broken your leg you would not expect to be able to go jogging immediately. Accept that time is essential and crucial in order for you to heal and mend. You have suffered a major trauma and it is not possible to place a set time-limit for recovery. The need for time and space is normal and natural; you are not weak or crazy. Regard yourself as a survivor not as a victim. Try to set aside some time each day, even if it is only 15 minutes; make it a priority. Regard it as yours and do as you want within that time span. It may be taking a bath, looking at a magazine, going for a walk, writing a letter, listening to music, or sitting and thinking. What you do with the time is less important than making sure that you have it, and using it as you would like. This is a useful exercise in regaining control and making choices.

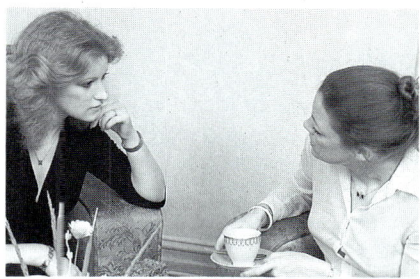

Above: *Sharing your feelings with a trusted friend or counsellor can help enormously in the recovery period.*

AT HOME AND AT WORK

Be realistic about what you can do. It is useful to have some stability in your life at this time, but try not to aim too high. Your confidence and self-esteem will grow just as well on small day-to-day successes. It can be useful to plan your day with breaks and rewards, especially if you find a particular chore very difficult. If help is offered, accept it, but do not let yourself and your life be 'taken over' by loving family and friends. It is important that you make decisions; even making small ones will help you to be in control of your life again.

If you work outside of the home, having some structure at work will be valuable. Try not to become overstressed and overworked. Again, if help is offered, accept it. You may find that you need some time away from work and if so take it without feeling guilty. If you live alone, try not to isolate yourself by refusing to see people.

SHARE YOUR FEELINGS

One of the most useful and healing ways of beginning again, after rape or sexual assault, is to talk about your feelings. It is best to do this with someone you trust and who cares about you. Try not to analyse the feelings too much as they will probably be different from day to day. Accept that you will have many contradictory thoughts and feelings during this time. Sharing the way you feel, both the pain and the successes, is a strong and brave thing to do. It is not weak to need other people. Speaking of the way you feel and of your reactions will help you to feel less isolated and more in control.

RAPE CRISIS CENTRES — WHAT THEY OFFER

They will always *listen*, however long ago you were attacked. The service is free and totally confidential. Rape Crisis groups exist in many areas and are always run by women.

If you contact a Rape Crisis Centre they will not tell the police, nor will they pressurize you to report if you do not want to. You will be supported in whatever decision you make. They give practical advice and information regarding medical and legal matters, where to go for pregnancy prevention after rape, pregnancy testing, abortion or adoption, and testing and treatment of sexually transmitted diseases.

Information is also available from them regarding financial compensation from the Criminal Injuries Compensation Board. In the USA, information can be obtained from the National Organization for Victim Assistance, in Washington DC. Over and above all of this, they provide immediate non-judgmental crisis counselling and ongoing counselling and support, for as long as you decide you need it.

TAKING CARE OF YOURSELF

This is a time to be gentle with yourself. By being self-indulgent and pampering yourself both physically and psychologically, you are saying that you matter and are worthwhile. 'Treating' yourself is also a good way of saying that you are important. Nurture yourself and allow others to nurture you. Try to be kind to your body; it has been hurt and invaded, as has your mind. Relaxation tapes may be useful to calm you and to help you to go to sleep. It is wise to seek medical advice about possible pregnancy, sexually transmitted diseases and any other injuries. Dealing with these will help you to feel in charge of your life.

REGAINING CONTROL

One of the best ways to feel in control of your life again is to take some action and to make some choices about safety.

Above: *A spy hole in your front door allows you to see your visitors and decide whether or not you wish to invite them in.*

SAFETY IDEAS

☐ Buy a screechy alarm.

☐ Be alert and know what is going on around you.

☐ Look people in the eye.

☐ Invest in a safety chain and a spy hole.

☐ Refuse to let callers in if you feel uneasy.

☐ Put your initial only on the door bell rather than your full name.

☐ Outside, walk quickly and assertively.

☐ Buy a porch light that switches on automatically if anyone walks near it.

☐ Join a self-defence class or take up a martial art.

☐ Find a like-minded friend and practise together some of the self-defence techniques in this book — whichever suit you the best.

☐ Write down some other things you can do to help you to feel safer.

Remember to use psychological self-defence and always be assertive. This anonymous poem has a message for us all:

I am thinking of a woman who walked into the waters
of a river with stones in her pockets
I am thinking of the waters of the rivers of my life
I am thinking of the stones in my pockets
All women are born with stones in their pockets
Empty them. Empty them. Empty them. Swim!

CHAPTER TWO

·SELF·DEFENCE·IS· ·NO·OFFENCE·

IN 1985 A SURVEY FOUND THAT OF 1236 LONDON WOMEN from all walks of life, one in six had been raped. One in three said that they had been either raped or sexually assaulted in other ways — which, as we shall see later, can be as bad as or even worse than being raped. Many women had been through such an experience more than once.

The only other survey at all comparable to the one in London was conducted in San Francisco, and it found an even higher rate of assault: 44% of the women said they had been through a rape or a rape attempt (Russell, *Rape in Marriage*). Reports from women on every continent confirm that the story is similar in most places round the world.

It is staggering to learn that rape is happening on such a massive scale. It is also heartening that so much is now being revealed. Over the last ten years of campaigning, Women Against Rape have seen women speaking out in an unprecedented way about what has happened to them — sometimes many years before. Rape is still not easy to talk

Previous page: *In August 1977 members of the WAR movement unfurled their banner at the feet of the Greek goddess Athena when they invaded the exclusive, all-male Athenaeum Club in Pall Mall, London, to which one of the judges in the Guardsman case belonged. They burst in on a dinner and handed out leaflets saying, 'Judges be warned! We will seek out your every hiding place.'*

SOME VITAL STATISTICS

Above: *A survey carried out in America concluded that women who struggle and fight back stand a better chance of avoiding rape.*

about, and most rape survivors are anonymous even to each other. But in this past decade women have made what was once a shameful secret a matter of increasing public anger and action, and this is true in many countries, both metropolitan and Third World.

Where rape has been accepted as a 'fact of life' which we can do little about, women in all sorts of situations are organizing to prevent it, and insisting on the social changes which will bring it to an end. Where it has been dismissed as a 'personal problem' for the woman who has been raped, more and more people are acknowledging that it is also society's problem. While a great deal of rape has for centuries been passed over as 'fun and games' which went 'a little over the top', women are more and more ready to protest at all sorts of sexual coercion. Collectively and as individuals, women are insisting on the right to relate to men as, when and if they so choose, resisting both sexual pressure and sexual assault.

One in five women in the London survey — more women than had been raped — had succeeded in fighting off a rapist, or in some way preventing a rape attempt. In the USA, figures published in 1986 by the Bureau of Justice Statistics show that a majority of the women threatened by a rapist had managed to fight off the attack, even when the rapist had a weapon. Of those threatened with a gun, 51% had prevented the rape; 58% when facing a knife; and when the rapist was unarmed, 72% had successfully resisted the assault.

One obstacle we face in fighting rape, alone or together, is a lack of information. No government has done the sensitive research necessary to find out how many women are raped, where, by whom, and how; the low priority given to gathering this vital information is evidence of the undervaluing of women's lives. Most statistics are based on cases reported to the police, which we now know to be a tiny minority. Therefore we must turn to our own research.

The London survey referred to in these pages was conducted by Women Against Rape (WAR), a campaigning organization founded in 1975, now part of the Wages for Housework Campaign. It was carried out because of the absence of basic statistical information on all aspects of rape. The full findings are reported in a book, *Ask Any Woman: A London inquiry into rape and sexual assault*, by Ruth Hall. We have space for only a small proportion of them here. Conducted by women for women, the survey is in many ways the first of its kind in the world, covering everything from verbal harassment in the street to rape inside marriage and racist sexual assault. Two thousand self-completion 16-page questionnaires were distributed to a wide variety of London women in shopping streets, bus queues, street markets, summer fairs, ante-natal clinics, hospital wards, pensioners' clubs, colleges, toddlers' one o'clock clubs, and bingo queues. Women's response was overwhelming: relief and excitement that finally someone wanted to know. And the high response rate, with 62% returned, adds weight to the results.

The survey found that the truth about rape has little to do with the stereotypes of rape mythology.

Readers of popular newspapers are informed every day that most rape is committed by a stranger in a dark alleyway; the picture is embellished by a description of the rapist as 'dark', 'swarthy', 'rough-looking', or 'scarred'.

The reality is that the rapist is not usually a stranger. Very often he is the woman's own husband, and we will see later how prevalent rape is inside marriage, and how this sets the scene for rape elsewhere. But even outside marriage, most rapists were not strangers. They were friends and workmates, boyfriends and ex-boyfriends, men in a position of authority over the woman or girl, members of her family, acquaintances, or others who knew her. Three out of four had raped a woman whom they knew.

Research in other countries has shown the same general pattern. In the San Francisco survey about three-quarters of the women who had been through rape or attempted rape said it had been by someone they knew. In a smaller New Zealand study, four-fifths of the women who had been raped knew their attackers. The Canadian Association of Sexual Assault Centres says that one woman in four will be raped some time in her life, most often by someone she knows.

Hidden under the imagery of a dark and/or poorly dressed rapist is the truth: that there is no 'type' of man more likely than others to rape. The media's implication that black men and poor men are more likely to be rapists is racist, and misleading to women, black and white. A white, clean-shaven face and a business suit do not mean safety: witness the stories which reach the press of rape and sexual assault by doctors, dentists, professors, psychiatrists, headmasters, estate agents, diplomats, and even priests. For every such case which comes to light, how many more such upstanding citizens go free under cover of their unassailable respectability? As this is being written, women in Philadelphia are fighting a hospital's reinstatement of a neurosurgeon whom no less than seven women patients have accused of sexual assault.

Such men have at their disposal many means of coercion. While they are not above brute force and physical violence, they can also force 'consent' or ensure the woman's silence by virtue of their position. Employers can threaten loss of a job or promotion prospects; teachers or professors can make a woman pass or fail; psychiatrists see us at our weakest, open to all kinds of emotional pressure; landlords can evict, and they have keys to women's flats or rooms.

Just as false as the media's stereotyped 'photofit' of the rapist is that of the 'type of woman' who makes a credible 'rape victim': the young, attractive blonde, in her late teens or twenties, single, heterosexual, and respectably employed. Any woman or girl can be raped, and if anything we are likely to be singled out not for fitting the media's definition of 'attractiveness', but for something about us or our situation that makes us vulnerable. Rapists are attracted to vulnerability.

Older women are, to varying degrees, at a physical disadvantage, often compounded by living alone, and by poverty which deprives them of the safer means of transport and security measures for their homes.

'THREE OUT OF EVERY FOUR RAPISTS RAPED A WOMAN THEY KNEW'

WHAT KIND OF WOMAN?

Very young women, meanwhile, are easier targets for moral blackmail and persuasion ('all the other girls do it'); in *Ask Any Woman* many women tell of how these pressures and inexperience can land you in impossible situations. Young women are also likely to have very little money. One woman in a 1977 speech described her dilemma:

'If you're going with a bloke — he has more money than you — you are dependent on him to take you places. And that means quite often you will have sex with him when you don't really want to — but just to keep him keen on you.

It may not be rape but it's not free choice either. If you go dancing, to a disco, the men will buy you drinks — but you have to weigh up what you're going to be asked to do in return later. And whether the bloke will take you home safely . . . or whether you're safer to walk through the streets on your own.'

A woman in this situation would be told in court that she was at least 'partly to blame', having 'led the man on' by going out with him. Yet *not* going out with men can also mean danger. Lesbian women may be singled out as fair game for sexual violence.

Women apply enormous ingenuity, determination, experience and skill to the job of preventing rape and other assault. Just how much expertise is involved can be seen immediately when we are away from home and have to struggle to learn quickly the information we need in order to survive. Women who are travelling, or are immigrants, either from another country or from countryside to city, may find themselves at a disadvantage from not knowing the language, or body language, not knowing the 'rules of the game' for conducting ordinary business, or simply from not knowing the times of the last bus home.

RACIST SEXUAL ASSAULT

Immigrant women, and many others, are afraid of being singled out for attack if they are 'different', particularly if their look or dress identifies them as women low in the social hierarchy. In *Ask Any Woman* many black women report that they have been sexually assaulted because of their race or nationality.

'There's a particular fear of white men that black girls grow up with. We know they think we're hot, sexual animals, that we're always available. It goes back to slavery. What they think about us sexually is part of the racism.'

One in eight women of African or Asian descent reported racist sexual assault, and more than one in five reported racist sexual verbal abuse. As the general level of racist attacks rises, and whole neighbourhoods, black and white, are terrorized, for instance, by gangs of extreme right-wing young men, the level of racist sexual assault is bound to increase. This is something experienced by both adults and children, and like other vulnerable sections of society, black women usually do not have the financial resources to afford cars or secure housing which might reduce the danger.

Whoever she is, a woman who is raped is likely to be accused of in some way 'asking for it'. Where another kind of physical assault would be taken seriously, rape survivors may find police officers exchanging knowing glances as soon as they hear that there was a 'sexual element'. Not only the police, but lawyers, jurors, judges, and sometimes even the woman's own friends and family, are liable to be suspicious, and more dismissive of rape than of a beating or robbery causing far less long-term damage. Questions like 'What were you doing out at that time of night?' are often aimed at establishing that since the assault was sexual, the woman really wanted it.

The accusation of 'asking for it' or 'leading the man on' is often used against women who choose to lead sexually active lives; the woman's sexual history, and her current boyfriend or boyfriends, may be dragged into a court case and frequently discredit her in the jury's eyes (Hall, James, and Kertész, *The Rapist Who Pays the Rent*). Still more damning are accusations that a woman works or has worked in some sexual occupation: prostitution, stripping, modelling, or even as a barmaid. Some prostitute women have managed to successfully prosecute men who have raped or sexually assaulted them. But it is hard to get the police to take such a case to court, and once you are there the judge is often unsympathetic. One judge, for instance, told a stripper that in her case the rape would do 'no lasting harm' (Women Against Rape, *Women at W.A.R.*, p. 15). Any woman can be called a prostitute, even a woman who is not in a sexual job at all, and many rapists go free as a result. Recent cases not only of rape but of murder have shown how the authorities' dismissive reaction to assaults on prostitutes puts *every* woman in added danger. (For example, the Yorkshire Ripper in Britain, the Southside Slayer in Los Angeles, and other multiple murderers.)

Most women at least sometimes find ourselves outside the definition of the 'blameless', 'respectable', victim. We can be accused of 'asking for' rape by being out at night, or living in or passing through the 'wrong' part of town; by having a relationship or relationships outside marriage; by being divorced, or dating a man, or getting into his car; by hitchhiking, by drinking, by dressing or behaving in a 'provocative', 'aggressive' or 'masculine' manner, or a 'sexy' 'feminine' manner, or even for the way we walk. But while women are accused of provoking rape by our situation or behaviour, the most traditionally respectable behaviour in the 'safest' environment does not provide immunity. No one could find any fault with the vicar's daughter raped in London in 1986 by three intruders who had knocked on the vicarage door.

'ASKING FOR IT'

Below: *17 July 1986: masked picket of the US Embassy, London, protesting the failure of Los Angeles police to catch the killer of at least 17 women, most of them young black women, described (often wrongly) by police as prostitutes. Women in five countries took action that day in support of LA's Black Coalition Fighting Back Serial Murders.*

The fear of rape places intolerable limitations on women's lives. It affects both major and minor decisions which should be ours alone: should I go to that party? Should I enrol for an evening class? Do I dare to go camping? tour Europe? leave my boyfriend? live alone? 'come out' in a lesbian relationship? allow my daughter — or son — to go for a walk in the woods? take an evening job? Independence, self-confidence, and knowledge of the world seem to come 'naturally' to most men and are identified as male qualities, as evidence that men are naturally more capable than women. The truth is that nature has nothing to do with it. All the circumstances of a woman's life conspire to set boundaries on what we can attempt, and undermine our self-confidence. Rape and the fear of rape reinforce the effects of financial dependence, overwork, and second-class treatment.

'YES MEANS YES, NO MEANS NO

HOWEVER WE DRESS AND WHEREVER WE GO'

Just as common as rape is women's resistance to it, which in recent years has become increasingly organized, visible, and worldwide.

In 1977 WAR held a Women's Rape Trial in Trafalgar Square, central London: a trial with a woman judge, a woman prosecutor and defence spokeswoman, and literally dozens of women who stepped forward to accuse those responsible for their rape. The trial followed a case where a 17-year-old woman was attacked by a soldier, Queen's Guardsman Thomas Holdsworth, who broke her ribs, tore her earlobes, and rammed a ring-covered fist into her vagina. The law in Britain defines 'rape' as 'sexual intercourse' (penile penetration) without the woman's consent. But this attack was a horrific example of how sexual assault using fists, or bottles, or oral or anal sex, can be just as devastating. When three Appeal Court judges overturned the soldier's prison sentence to protect his 'promising army career', the young woman went to the press with her story, and later brought the case to the Women's Court in Trafalgar Square.

Cases like that of the guardsman have naturally focussed women's anger on the State, first on the courts, then on the police, and finally on the government. WAR first came to prominence by invading a court and chasing out one of the Holdsworth judges, and we have written elsewhere about the changes needed in the law, court procedures and government policy. Here we focus rather on specific demands put forward by women in all sorts of situations to make women's safety a priority and a recognized responsibility of those in charge.

REFUSING RAPE IN WAGED WORK

Access to waged jobs, including those identified as 'men's jobs' which are almost always higher paid, has been one of the basic demands of the women's movement. But the threat of rape and sexual assault can be an obstacle to many jobs even when other barriers have been overcome. One issue is the safety of the premises.

On 17 January 1980 at 3 a.m. a black woman worker was raped and beaten in the women's toilets at a General Electrics plant in Lynn, Massachusetts. She was the only woman among the fifty or so employees working the late shift in that building. The women's room, one level up from the main floor, was so far from the work area that screams could not be heard. As one woman worker described it, the ladies' toilets 'were obviously an afterthought with no consideration as to their safety'. In fury, men and women employees formed a safety committee, organized a public meeting, and gathered the support of a wide range of women's, black and community organizations. Together they wrote to the company:

> We the undersigned hold you, General Electric, responsible for . . . providing a working environment for women free of the threat of sexual assault . . . If the company can afford to burn Christmas lights night and day, they can afford better lighting in and around buildings and the parking lots.

Women who are raped or sexually assaulted when intruding on men's job territory do not always find such solid support. In fact the offenders often *are* a woman's workmates. Such was the case in London when a firewoman — one of only five in the city — was tied to a ladder, hosed with powerful jets of water, forced to watch her colleagues expose themselves, and more, in an 'initiation ritual'. When she complained, firemen rallied to the defence of their seven male colleagues who faced disciplinary action. Amid grumbles about how women should not be allowed in the fire brigades, there were threats of a strike if any of the men were fired. In the event only one man was, and he was later reinstated.

In 'women's jobs' putting up with such assaults is sometimes an unwritten part of the job description. The sexual demands on secretaries are no less real for being caricatured daily in comic strips round the world, which are full of pretty young women being chased around desks by leering executives. Sexual services are often part of the personal care and attention expected of the 'office wife'. Women in jobs

serving or caring for members of the public (e.g. waitresses, nurses and teachers) also face a high level of sexual abuse and assault. And most vulnerable of all are those who work as maids, cleaners, nannies or au pairs in other people's houses — still one of the major forms of employment for women, both in metropolitan and Third World countries. Clotil Walcott, Chairperson of the National Union of Domestic Employees (NUDE) in Trinidad and Tobago reports that many 'such women workers end up with an unwanted child . . . as part of her payment from an unscrupulous boss or one of his drunken friends.' (Walcott, *Fight Back Says a Woman*, p. 5.)

Among women who once would have had no hope of redress, who would have left the job in silence or stayed on at the cost of their physical and mental health, some now speak out and fight the case. Women's independent organizing has led to the formation of groups which deal specifically with sexual harassment. Lawyers have been brought in to apply civil rights and sex discrimination legislation. Videos, films, pamphlets, speakouts and surveys have revealed the issue to the public eye, and many trade unions have also taken action, sometimes setting up special grievance procedures for sexual abuse.

Like workers in 'men's jobs', women in traditional occupations like nursing have had to fight for the safety of their premises. For nurses this often means not only the hospitals, but their own homes and hostels,

Below: *Nurses from Hammersmith Hospital in West London requested lessons in self-defence from a black belt judo instructor, after some of them had been attacked in the nearby streets when returning home from late duty.*

which have always been an attractive target for rapists. In pouring rain, more than seventy student nurses from Port of Spain General Hospital in Trinidad demonstrated outside the office of the Prime Minister to protest the lack of security which led to rape in a student nurses' hostel in November 1985; a man had climbed in through a window at three in the afternoon. At a torchlit vigil which followed, it was Clotil Walcott, representing domestic employees, who came to support the nurses while middle-class feminists failed to turn up until it was over.

Two weeks later another nurse was raped in a ward of the same hospital; when the chief security officer refused to do anything about it she decided to sue the Ministry of Health. The Trinidad nurses' determination to get adequate protection was echoed in 1986 by student nurses at St Mary's Hospital, London, who threatened a sit-in at the hospital's main entrance in support of their demands for security patrols and a safer nurses' home.

One victory of collective organizing in waged workplaces is that men have often been mobilized to support women working at their side, although this is not always straightforward. At General Electric, Massachusetts, a woman on the safety committee reports that 'many of the male workers probably think we shouldn't be in a big dirty place like this — some comments have been made about how we should be at home taking care of the kids'. Yet the men reacted to what happened with fury and determination to make the management accountable. It was a male GE machinist who said,

MEN AGAINST RAPE

'A rape occurred on the GE property during working hours. They have not explained anything to us. They should be made to bleed until we get some answers.'

He clearly took it personally. And so, on the other side of the country, did the 1400 woodworkers, all but 50 of them male, who struck for eight weeks against a company in Washington State where the supervisor sexually propositioned new women recruits. 'We have some staunch strong male chauvinists in this union and some will always be that way,' said the president of the local branch, who led the IWA union dispute. But as a result of the strike 'a lot of [the men] have changed their opinion about women in the workplace and feel they should be given a fair shot.'

Feminist writing and organizing on rape has not always been open even to the possibility of men's support. One well-known book on rape, Susan Brownmiller's *Against Our Will*, holds that 'By anatomical fiat — the inescapable construction of their genital organs — the human male was a natural predator and the human female served as his natural prey.' Men are naturally predators and women naturally victims!

In contrast to this pessimistic and reactionary acceptance of pre-destination, some men have themselves sought to identify the forces which make men into rapists. In 1977, Payday, a men's network against all unpaid work which operates with and in support of the Wages for Housework Campaign, wrote in consultation with WAR in support of our Rape Trial, and of the women-only march which brought us to Trafalgar Square:

> Guardsman Holdsworth's defence used the fact that he was a soldier to get him off. The Court of Appeal confirmed that violence was expected of him, as a soldier and as a man. Men in uniform — soldiers, police — represent what is expected of all men. We are all expected to be experts in violence. That means we are expected to have power and authority over women, to use violence or the threat of violence first of all against *them* . . .
>
> The more women are financially independent of men, the easier it will be for men to refuse to play the policeman and foreman, in marriage or in the street, at home or abroad.
>
> Moreover, all of us know that only to the degree that women are financially independent of men can we be sure that our relationships with women are voluntary on their part.

There is no space here to do more than mention the many other places where women have organized, often successfully, in self-defence. The colleges and universities where charges of sexual harassment by teachers have been proved and in the USA have led to professors being fired; where students have occupied buildings to demand and win better lighting and security in dorms and grounds, alarm systems, and free night mini-buses for women students. Public transport where women have fought cuts in services or staff, because every cut means

Below: *Better Lighting In The Streets was formed by the residents of the London suburb of Surbiton after a series of rapes. They staged this protest in November 1984.*

more women raped and imposes a curfew on many women (in the USA one woman sued the railway responsible for security at the station where she and many others had been raped, and won $750,000 compensation). The streets where, even in 'leafy suburban areas', women have organized pressure groups for better lighting; where around the world women have held massive torchlight processions 'taking back the night'. Council housing estates and other public housing where women have demanded lights, locks and entryphones, and where pressure has meant that some local authorities (for instance Camden, London, where WAR is based) now consult women's and black community organizations on ways to prevent sexual and racial assaults.

The most common setting of all for rape is inside marriage. The *Ask Any Woman* survey found that of respondents who were or had been formally married, *one in seven* had been raped by their own husbands — which means that in any London street there must be several homes where rape is, or has been, a part of married life. Counting common-law marriage, rape in marriage was found to be more frequent than all other rape combined.

RAPE IN MARRIAGE

The San Francisco study we have referred to earlier similarly found that one in seven married women said a husband had raped or attempted to rape her. In Germany a rape study conducted by a popular magazine found an even higher rate: 18% or 64% of married women (depending on the definition used). In Australia a major women's magazine found that 1% of *all* women had suffered marital rape.

Marriage puts at a man's disposal a whole battery of ways of coercing his wife, especially when she is financially dependent. Our survey showed how moral and emotional blackmail can vary from accusations of being 'unreasonable, frigid, mean,' etc. to threats of suicide. Along with all the other service work of a wife, sex is still widely considered a duty, in return for the income that the husband is expected to bring in. A woman who cares for children 18 hours a day and gets up at night for the baby, is still considered to 'owe' something to the breadwinner of the family (she 'doesn't work'). And men often use violence to enforce these 'conjugal rights'. In *Ask Any Woman* one woman said:

> 'My husband's behaviour was continually threatening and violent throughout the nine years of marriage. Sex was a constant area of violence and abuse. I was too frightened to refuse him most of the time.'   .

In Britain and most countries, rape in marriage is legal — perhaps the most important statement the law makes about women. In a book on the consequences of this law WAR reports how women have described, the 'unimaginable physical pain, like having a crowbar rammed into my body', the degradation, the 'sense of defilement' and abuse, their revulsion, the nervous state to which the rape reduces them, the fear of recurrence, and in many cases the sense of being trapped without an escape route, without recognition of what they are suffering, and without recourse to the law (*The Rapist Who Pays the Rent*).

All women are affected by the rape in marriage law.

> The legality of rape in marriage assumes that a woman's body is not her own . . . This assumption is present in *every* rape case, undermining natural justice (*The Rapist Who Pays the Rent*, p. 20).

'NO, NO, BECOMING A WIFE DOESN'T MEAN "YES" FOR THE REST OF YOUR LIFE'

Women have now succeeded in making rape in marriage illegal in much of Australia, in Canada, in many Eastern European countries including the USSR, and in the Scandinavian countries. In Scotland in 1982 a judge ruled that it is 'in modern times illogical and unreasonable' to treat rape as different from other assault in marriage.

In the USA there are more states every year where husbands are told it is no longer legal to rape their wives. And the laws are working. In California, for instance, where rape in marriage was criminalized in 1980, 56 cases had been brought by 1983. Forty-three ended in conviction, a very high conviction rate of 75%.

Women are now pressing for a change in the law where it has not yet been established that our bodies are our own. At the same time we are fighting, individually and together, for the resources which must accompany the law if it is to be effective.

Most women who are being raped in their marriage try to leave, but are prevented, especially when they have children, by having 'no money and no place to go'. In some cases the man wields his financial power openly, holding back on the rent or the housekeeping money if he doesn't get his 'conjugal rights'. In others, the woman's and children's financial dependence may work more subtly to set the terms of the relationship. Women have combatted this by taking waged jobs, to have a little money to call their own. Welfare too has been an important weapon enabling women to leave the marriage, and the vast and growing numbers of mothers and other women on supplementary benefit (welfare) reflect in large measure a refusal of rape. So too does the women's refuge movement, where women put up with horrendous overcrowding in order to escape from violent husbands; in the refuge they can to some extent protect each other.

WOMEN COUNT, COUNT WOMEN'S WORK

At the same time, women are challenging the lack of recognition which puts them in such a vulnerable position in the first place, at home and elsewhere. ILO statistics show that women do two-thirds of the world's work (twice as much as men) for 5% of the income and 1% of the assets. The value of much of this work, including housework, childcare and (particularly but not only in Third World countries) farm work, has never been quantified. Since much of our work brings us no wages and no recognition, it is not surprising that women are seen as less valuable members of society than men. Women's word counts for less, women's pain counts for less, and women's safety is less of a priority, in marriage, in the law, and in court.

The relationships which are based on this invisible work are so ingrained that they are taken to be 'human nature'. Just as rape is said to be due to the 'nature' of men, caring for others is said to come 'naturally' to women. When a husband demands sexual services regardless of the wishes of his wife, when a man on a date becomes insistent, when a boss puts pressure on a secretary, it is all put down to 'human nature' and women are 'naturally' expected to comply.

For these reasons, married and unmarried women are now organizing together to insist on recognition, and a wage, for their labour. Already the United Nations, at the end of its Decade for Women, agreed after lobbying by women that all women's work should be measured and counted in every country's gross national product.

Women in many countries are working to get governments to implement this decision. One of the first and most urgent effects will be to lend force to the efforts of millions of women to establish that they will not be slaves in the office or the bedroom, and to build relationships with men that both can enjoy.

If it is hard for women to speak out about rape in marriage, it is even harder for children to say what is happening to them, inside or outside the family. It is only recently, in the context of the women's anti-rape movement, that the scale of rape and sexual assault against girls, and sometimes boys, has begun to be exposed. A staggeringly high number of women in *Ask Any Woman* said they had been raped or sexually assaulted when they were girls, and this is confirmed daily by other investigations and by cases now being reported. The survey also showed how very difficult it is for girls and young women to speak out. Whom can they tell? What will be the repercussions? Will they be believed? What if the offender is the girl's stepfather or her brother?

It is one of the major breakthroughs of the anti-rape movement that more children and young people are now finding the strength to take action and are finding more adults prepared to listen. In some countries there are now the first networks of emergency phone lines and refuges for children. And, most important, it is beginning to be established that children too have the right to say 'no' to unwanted touching — a revolutionary idea being applied not only to men in dirty raincoats, but to grandparents, uncles and aunts!

In important ways resistance is now becoming harder for young people: unemployment, for instance, may mean increased dependence on a father or stepfather who demands a price in physical as well as emotional services. In Britain, 'bed and breakfast' legislation, shortages of housing, and the low level of benefits are forcing young women and men back 'home' to families which many had strong reasons to escape, and which in any case reduce their status yet again to that of children.

At the same time, however, many children are now being taught in school the first principle of self-defence: that their bodies belong to them alone and not to any adult who wants to touch, hold or kiss them. In watching or acting out real-life situations, they practise firm refusals, try out screaming, consider whom to tell, and gain a little confidence that with luck and perseverance, their word will count for as much as the man's. It is a sign of the times that you can turn on the television and see a classroom full of five-year-olds singing: 'My body's nobody's body but mine. You run your own body, let me run mine.'

'NOBODY'S BODY BUT MINE'

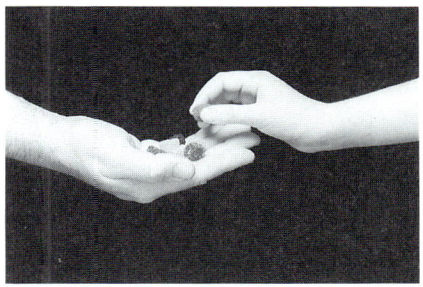

Above: *In primary schools children are now encouraged to believe that their bodies belong to them, and that they have the right to say 'No' to anyone, and should never accept a bribe.*

THE ART OF SELF-DEFENCE

Above: *By joining martial arts or self-defence classes, women can learn to protect themselves effectively.*

TO SUIT OUR NEEDS

One method women have found for preventing rape is to learn to defend themselves physically. Recent years have seen a mushrooming of self-defence classes of all sorts, from the one-off demonstration of basic techniques, to martial arts training to which women commit themselves for years. Demand for these classes comes from women with a wide variety of different reasons for feeling vulnerable to attack: different physical abilities; different ages, races, relationships with men, other women and children; different financial resources, means of transport, homes; different experiences of assault or of frightening events.

Women who have already been raped or assaulted very often turn to self-defence as a way of dealing with the disabling fear which can follow an attack. A major part of the meaning of rape is power. The woman is made to feel helpless, unable to defend even that which is most private. Gaining the physical skills to prevent it happening next time is a way of reversing the humiliating sense of powerlessness which is one of rape's lasting effects. Some women end up feeling stronger than they did before they were attacked.

One reason women have often been reluctant to let people know they have been raped is the fear that they will then be identified as a 'rape victim'. The label 'victim' is a reminder that the woman was unable to prevent something terrible from happening to her. Women have increasingly moved away from the term 'victim' to identify themselves as 'rape survivors' — people who have *come through* an ordeal. At the same time, they have organized rape crisis centres to help deal with the after-effects. For many women self-defence training is the key to moving from victim to survivor.

The martial arts, as presently taught and practised, depend on the development of a high level of physical strength, flexibility, balance, stamina and speed. These may not be possible for women who are pregnant, for example, or who have multiple sclerosis. Yet women who are pregnant, older women, and women with disabilities can benefit from training. Those who cannot run, knock out an assailant, or resist a determined assault indefinitely may still be able to use some forms of self-defence to increase their chances and their self-confidence. They have a right to training which is *accessible, affordable, and adapted to their physical needs*. There can be no excuse for lack of provision, in courses, for those women who for one reason or another may need them the most.

For pregnant women assault can be particularly devastating, as one woman reported to the *Ask Any Woman* survey:

'My youngest son was born premature. He was very ill and is deaf.'

Older women worry that for them any assault may mean the end of their independence, or even their life.

Women of all ages who have a disability may worry about how an assault would affect them physically, and undermine the survival skills they have carefully worked out to manage independently from day to day. A disability can single you out as an easy target, not likely to strike back, and often without the social power to do anything about the attack afterwards.

WinVisible, an organization of women with visible and invisible disabilities, say:

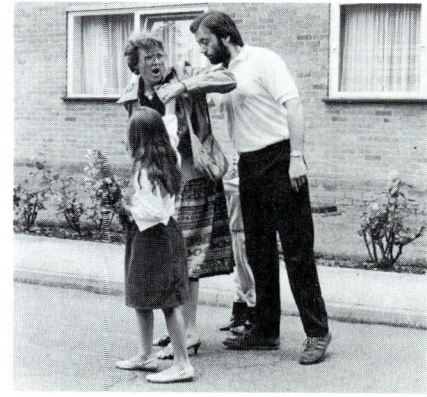

Above: *Women with small children often feel particularly vulnerable to assault, or simply to unwanted attentions from men. Not only do they have to protect themselves, but their children too. Saying 'Go away' confidently and without fear is a useful form of self-defence that all of us can learn.*

Due to lack of access and resources, we are forced to ask for a variety of help, e.g. having to be lifted, having to use a goods lift with a male staff member, having to accept a push from strangers, or a hand down from a bus, or frequently ask directions. Genuine offers of help are hard to distinguish from offers of help used as a pretext. Some women with disabilities avoid help in order to avoid possible harassment. Transport schemes for people with disabilities carry their own risk, where women are alone with male drivers. In Dial-A-Ride vans, wheelchair users are clamped in one spot for safety. Complaints have not been taken seriously by those who could discipline the drivers concerned, since women with disabilities are sometimes supposed not to know what is going on, and are not to be believed, one reason being the stereotype of the sexually frustrated woman with a disability.

Training may mean that a woman who is pregnant, elderly, ill, or a wheelchair user is able to enhance her ability to shout for help, or that she feels prepared enough and strong enough in herself to talk her way out. It may be possible to intimidate and confuse an assailant, for instance by chanting, shouting, silence, or pretence; to fend off a 'helper' who is taking advantage of a brief opportunity; or to resist long enough to buy time until someone else appears or the assailant gives up and goes away. This is not so different from the position any woman may find herself in, whatever her physical abilities, especially when she faces a gun, a knife, a gang of men, or a locked door.

Older women, and women with disabilities, can and do send assailants fleeing in shock and surprise, and for some women being prepared to do this is an important part of how they feel about their lives. As one woman told the *Ask Any Woman* survey:

'My experiences have left me embittered and determined to defend any aged and physically handicapped people — especially myself!'

Girls too can sometimes be effective despite their size. In February 1986 for example, police asked London hospitals to be on the lookout for a man aged 40—50 and around 5'10" tall, seeking treatment for a dislocated shoulder. A 13-year-old girl, of 5'2" and trained in judo, had sent him flying over her head.

As she threw him aside she felt his shoulder blade come out and he screamed with pain (*Daily Telegraph*, 3 February 1986).

'EVERY MAN I MEET WANTS TO PROTECT ME. CAN'T IMAGINE WHAT FROM.'
(Mae West)

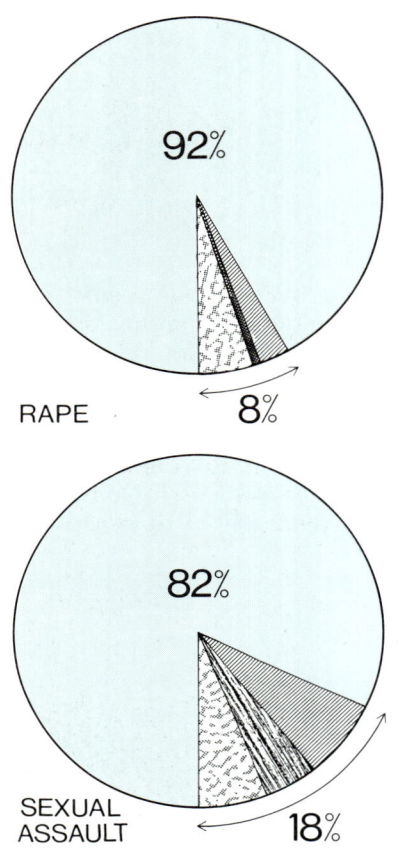

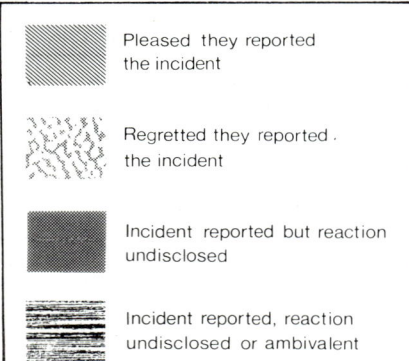

Above: *The WAR enquiry into rape and sexual assault in London, carried out in 1982, found that only 8 per cent of women who had been raped reported it to the police. Of the women who had experienced sexual assault only 18 per cent reported it.*

One of the greatest satisfactions for women studying self-defence is that they are on the whole no longer dependent on anyone else for protection. All our lives we are told we should have a man to 'take care of us': quite a funny idea really, since many women spend their lives taking care of both children and men.

Depending on men for protection has serious drawbacks. Having to make elaborate arrangements to be collected or accompanied limits where many women can go, and how often. It also affects the relationship with whoever is doing the fetching: however obliging the man may be, he's still the strong one generously doing you a favour. Depending on men can also be risky. It is not uncommon for a man who offers a woman a lift home to drive her off to a lonely spot instead. Knowing the man, even knowing him well, is no guarantee against this. Yorkshire women complained of this before the Ripper was caught. Even men who have intervened to stop a woman being assaulted have been known to take advantage of her distressed condition. And the statistics on rape in marriage and rape of girls in the family put the lie to the idea that home with your husband or father is the safest place to be. To learn a martial art is to challenge any dependence on this protection racket.

Equally, it is a victory for women not to be dependent on the protection of the police, who so often take the position that the safest thing for women is to limit their activities. There is a growing acknowledgement in Britain and many other countries that women are profoundly dissatisfied with the police response to rape. *Ask Any Woman* was able for the first time to put a figure on how few women who are raped report it to the police, and found it to be only *one in twelve*. (This is for cases other than rape in marriage which is rarely, if ever, reported.) Women explain what makes them reluctant to report, many feeling that because of their race, nationality, style of dress, sexual history, or other factors, they would not qualify as an 'appropriate victim'.

The fear of being unacceptable to the police is reinforced by a catch-22. On the one hand we are often urged not to resist a rapist because we might 'get hurt'. On the other hand, if we cannot show signs of a physical struggle, will anyone in authority believe we did not consent? In the absence of 'corroborative' cuts and bruises the police are often reluctant to press charges, and courts often will not convict.

Beginning the very day WAR's survey was published in January 1985, there has been a steady flow of news reports in Britain about new 'rape suites' in some police stations, with a more comfortable atmosphere. It is a major achievement for women that the police have acknowledged a need to change their ways, and are training officers to be more sympathetic. Yet a *Woman's Own* survey on rape in 1986 found that almost half the women who had reported rape recently were still being treated 'badly' or 'with no great compassion' (*Woman's Own*, 23 August 1986). Meanwhile WAR have been told that in many places increased expenditure on rape 'could not be justified' in the light of the low numbers of — reported — rapes! So long as this is the official approach most cases will continue to go unreported, and women will be left without the police protection from rape which we deserve and need to have.

In addition to their failure to make women's safety a priority, the police may not be safe company. Women say they have been subjected to sexual jokes and innuendo in the police station after reporting a rape. In fact it is not unknown for women to be raped or sexually assaulted *by* policemen.

Women have challenged such police behaviour in Britain, the USA, and other western countries. In Britain, two black women have recently spoken out in court: Esme Baker of London described being sexually assaulted in a police van, and Jackie Berkeley of Manchester told the court that she had been raped in a police station. In Chicago, USA, 191 women were awarded compensation for police strip searches in March 1980.

The place where women have most consistently tackled police rape is India. Forum Against Rape in Maharashtra State has documented a whole series of such cases, beginning with that of Mathura, over which thousands of women organized in 1980. A Forum leaflet opens:

Not rape, the Supreme Court said, it was only intercourse. Mathura, a 14 to 16-year-old farm labourer in a village in Maharashtra, 'willingly submitted' to sexual intercourse with Ganpat, a policeman she had never seen before. In the middle of the night. Near a police station latrine. Where the door was bolted and the lights put out.

Below: *In 1985 a young black woman, Jackie Berkeley, was put on trial for 'wasting police time' when she reported being raped in Moss Side police station, Manchester. Women Against Rape provided an expert witness for her defence. In London, Black Women for Wages for Housework and WAR picketed daily outside the Appeal Courts. She was found guilty and given a suspended prison sentence.*

Besides such individual assaults, mass rape by the police has been commonplace. Repression of a movement to reclaim land in a village in eastern Bihar, for instance, included police going from house to house burning, looting, beating and raping so brutally that some of the women died, including one woman raped just after delivering a baby. While the issue has been raised in the Indian Parliament, one authority has backed up another, and only the action of women themselves has brought world attention to this onslaught.

Forum Against Rape reports that 'for every reported rape there are ten to twelve unreported ones': the same proportion, roughly, as the one in twelve we found in London. Their 1980 statement concludes, 'Yes, there is safety in numbers. And strength. So let's change the balance. Join us.'

COLLECTIVE SELF-DEFENCE

As well as pressing the police and courts to act against rapists, the movement in India has exacted its own justice. In one case 'in Maharashtra, when an adivasi woman was raped by a landlord, the women of the village got together, held a trial presided over by the people. The culprit was paraded through the village and thus publicly humiliated.' And in Bombay, 'when news of a rape incident spread, more than 500 people gathered around the house of the rapist and demanded that he be punished.' (From a Forum leaflet.)

Collective actions of this kind serve as a way for the woman who has been raped to regain self-respect. But at the same time they are a form of pre-emptive self-defence, for her and for other women in the community. As a way of preventing this man (and others) from doing the same again, such actions are probably at least as effective as prison — and can also lead to a prison sentence where none would otherwise have resulted.

In other places too, women — sometimes together with men — have confronted rapists and wife-beaters with the strength of numbers. In villages in China for example, this has taken the form of 'people's courts'. *Fanshen*, the history of one village in the Chinese revolution, describes how the village Women's Association called in a man who had beaten his wife for going to their meetings, and 'rushed at him from all sides, knocked him down, kicked him, tore his clothes, scratched his face, pulled his hair and pummelled him' until he promised never to beat her again (Hinton, *Fanshen*, p. 185).

In the US groups of women have organized to go with a rape survivor and humiliate the rapist in a public place, such as a doctor's waiting room or a park. In some cases, avoiding face-to-face confrontation, women have spray-painted the word 'rapist' on the offender's home or car, or put up 'wanted' posters with his photograph, or printed lists of men indicted for sex offences for distribution all over the city and through the newspapers and radio. At the same time, collective self-defence has meant organizing *before* rape occurs: 'rape squads', whistle systems, schemes of safe houses in a neighbourhood. If no one else can or will protect them, women have prepared to protect themselves.

This is the climate in which increasing numbers of women are devoting their free time to martial arts training so that even when they are alone

SAFER STREETS

The measures London women considered most important to make the streets safer for women in order of priority are:

☐ Improved public transport

☐ More police attention to protection of women

☐ More street lighting

☐ Readily available self-defence classes

From *Ask Any Woman*, an enquiry into rape and sexual assault in London.

they will be able to stand their ground, without depending either on men or the police. One woman who rang the police when two men were breaking her door down says:

'I was trying desperately to ring the local police station, and when they eventually answered the PC quite simply did not believe what was happening. After a number of "Are you sure?" from the PC, I put the phone down and reached for the broomstick in my kitchen . . . I decided then that if the police were not defending me I could not count on good luck and therefore I had to do something to defend myself. . . . I was going to try some martial art.'

The increased safety which women martial arts experts achieve for themselves will also ultimately benefit other women. If present trends continue, rapists will soon have to regard every woman as a potentially dangerous customer.

How far can you go in self-defence without finding the police and legal system ranged *against* you?

THE RIGHT TO DEFEND YOURSELF

In the 1970s the cases of two black American women who had killed their assailants helped to establish, and popularize internationally, the principle that self-defence is no offence. Joan Little, a prisoner, killed one of her jailers after he raped her. A massive campaign was organized to defend her, and in 1975 she was acquitted. Inez Garcia shot a man after he helped another man rape her, and threatened her with further assault. She stated:

'I am not ashamed of what I have done. I was afraid and I had to defend myself. I would like other people to know about my case. I think they can identify with me. And if they have the same thing happen to them, they will know how I felt. Maybe it will stop more rapes.'

Originally jailed for murder, she was freed on appeal in 1977 by a jury which agreed that the shooting was a perfectly reasonable act of self-defence.

The slogan 'Self Defence Is No Offence' is now being used in many countries to support those who defend themselves, sometimes from rape, sometimes from other assaults. In Britain it was popularized by twelve young Asian men known as the Bradford Twelve, who had prepared petrol bombs to defend their community from an expected racial attack by right-wing extremists. When the attack did not materialize, the unused weapons were dumped, but the young men were later arrested and charged with 'conspiracy' crimes warranting life imprisonment.

The Bradford Twelve were acquitted in 1982, and their lawyer, Ruth Bundey, spelled out what the jury's decision also means for women and their right to defend themselves:

. . . the result of the trial for all of us is a fantastic breakthrough, because it established a legal basis for self-defence in a far wider way than had been possible before. And it also established the *necessity* for using self-defence where the State does not protect black people, or any people in society. It's a far cry from the trial some years ago of a woman called Sara Dixon in Bradford, who was charged with carrying an offensive weapon, which was a knife, at the time when the Yorkshire Ripper still hadn't been caught, when she lived very near to one of the victims . . . (James, *Strangers and Sisters*, p. 165).

The court's decision has since been reaffirmed in other cases involving petrol bombs — in one case made by tenants to defend themselves from eviction by a slum landlord's gang of hired thugs. But judgments have not been consistent, and some have gone against the principle of self-defence from racists' attacks, and the principle of women's right to carry self-defence weapons has not yet been established. In Britain, London's Metropolitan Police state:

A woman under attack has, of course, every right to defend herself with reasonable force . . . What the law does not allow is carrying anything which could be described as an 'offensive weapon'. This would include a specially adapted item such as a sharpened comb, or a knife, if carried for self-defence (Metropolitan Police, *Positive Steps*, p. 16).

In other words, *defensive* weapons are legally *offensive*, and women are forced to consider not only what is useful to carry but how they can justify having that item in their bag.

Nevertheless, the level of fear among women is so high that the *Ask Any Woman* survey found that a majority do carry weapons, or at least keep in mind other objects they are carrying; the list includes many bizarre and original ideas of what could be pressed into service in self-defence. Given the level of danger women face, and the lack of other protection, the choice of what to carry should belong to us.

The law as it stands in most English-speaking countries declares that appropriate self-defence is an absolute right, even if it results in the attacker's death. But women have problems in exercising this right.

Pre-emptive action may be the only way to be effective in self-defence against men who are bigger and stronger than ourselves. Part of martial arts training is learning to recognize signs of danger. Yet the law may not allow effective action until the moment of advantage is past and the attack has already begun. In 1979, after nine years' brutal battering, and having failed to get any help from the police, June Greig in Scotland fought back one day and killed her husband. Many battered women knew exactly what she meant when she said that on that day he hadn't beaten her yet, but she could tell by the look in his eyes he was coming after her. She was jailed for six years.

Above: *Cartoon from the Lawyers Collective, Bombay, India.*

The principle of a 'pre-emptive strike' is accepted for policemen. In October 1983, in the Stephen Waldorf case, London police opened fire on an unarmed man sitting in a car stuck in a traffic jam. They had mistaken him for another man, who was believed to be armed and dangerous, and the courts ruled that they had the right to fire first in self-defence, before any move or threatening gesture had been made against them. The same principle does not usually apply to women threatened with battering.

For a woman to injure anyone who has not yet injured her goes against a life-long training in compassion and self-denial. Yet at the beginning of an assault we cannot know what will happen next — whether we will be raped, or cut, or whether rape will turn to murder. Women are increasingly preparing themselves to take decisive action before it is too late, knowing that an early move may be our only chance.

The court may also fail to share a woman's point of view of just how serious rape itself is. An American article on the legal aspects of self-defence noted that 'case law . . . allows the use of deadly force to prevent forcible sodomy between males, but has not yet sanctioned a woman's right to use deadly force to repel a rape.' (*Heresies*, No. 6, 1978.) As one of the jurors in Inez Garcia's first trial explained, 'you can't kill someone for trying to give you a good time.'

CHANGING THE BALANCE

The place where women most commonly use serious violence in self-defence is the place where rape is legal: at home, within marriage. If it is hard for women to get police protection elsewhere, it can be nearly impossible when the assailant is the husband. Again and again women have documented how the police, called to bloody scenes of 'battering', refuse to take action on the grounds that they do not want to 'interfere' in a 'domestic dispute'.

In 1985 a Connecticut woman set an important precedent when she sued the police for failing to protect her, and won.

> Tracey Thurman, now 24, was left partially paralyzed in an attack by her ex-husband, who stabbed her 13 times and kicked her in the head in the presence of a police officer. Ms. Thurman had tried repeatedly to get police protection, file charges, and have her ex-husband arrested for assaults and threats on her life, but her complaints were rejected, ignored, or met with false promises by Torrington police . . .
> On June 25, 1985, a jury found that the police had violated Thurman's rights and also were negligent in handling the case, awarding her $2.3 million and her 3-year-old son, who witnessed the attack, $300,000 (*Out From Under*, Winter, 1986).

A MATTER OF LIFE AND DEATH

When the police have failed to provide protection, or when women have been unable to apply to them, there are wives who kill their husbands in self-defence. In some cases, hearing how the woman has lived through years of vicious brutality, fearing for her life and her children's, beaten when ill, beaten when pregnant, the courts are

Above: *Jogging is one way women take time for themselves — 'running out of the kitchen'. Running is also the first form of self-defence.*

RUNNING AWAY FROM RAPE

sympathetic. There is a growing list of wives who are acquitted on grounds of self-defence, or more often, convicted of manslaughter and set free without a prison sentence. Yet in other cases judge and jury respond with fury, and solidarity of man for man. Sentencing June Greig for her pre-emptive strike, Judge Dunpark explained 'it must be a long term of imprisonment not merely to punish her but to deter other wives in the same position from killing their husbands.'

A few years later, Iqbal Begum killed her husband with an iron bar after he beat her and threatened to murder two of their children. A black woman, facing an English court speaking no English and with no interpreter, she was sentenced to life imprisonment, in a murder trial lasting 15 minutes. An appeal was organized by a women's campaign on the grounds that self-defence is no offence, and in 1985 she was freed to rejoin her children after serving four years in jail.

Elsewhere we have compared such cases with the steady stream of husbands who, after killing their wives, not in self-defence and not after years of beatings but for unfaithfulness or 'nagging', are set free.

Physical violence, which husbands are so often permitted to use against their wives, reinforces women's subordination on questions like money, housework, and whose word goes. Women's relative physical weakness and the fact that, unlike boys, many of us grow up with no practice in sport or vigorous activities, mean that men can literally push us around. Many lives might be saved if more wives had the physical training to call a halt to brutality *before* it ends in death.

In less violent relationships too, training for a woman can make a big difference. A black belt in karate has told WAR that if there were any physical confrontation she could throw her husband over her shoulder, and he knows it: she's done it before. Even where the husband imposes his will by means of financial or emotional pressure, training can help to redress the power balance, just as, outside marriage, it can change the balance of power between a girl and her brother, or a woman on a date and a man to whom she would otherwise be forced to submit out of what one woman has described as 'my feminine niceness (i.e. fear)'.

For women, martial arts is the meeting point of two movements to regain control of their own bodies. One is the movement against rape and sexual harassment, and the fight for a sexual life which is not a duty but a joy, with women or with men. The other is the women's sports and fitness movement.

For generations women were supposed to pay attention to our bodies only to make them beautiful for men. Often working at two jobs, one at home and one outside, looking after everyone else's ailments, they have had little time or energy for their own health or fitness. Millions of women make a joke of how they are 'not allowed to get ill'. When we look for medical attention, it is another struggle to keep control of our treatment in our own hands, through establishing women's health centres and self-help groups, and through investigating an alternative and wholistic approach to health and nutrition. It is also a battle to control when, whether, and how we will have babies. Women's bodies sometimes feel more like a machine at the service of others than something of our own.

In this context choosing to do physical training is a victory. Many women train because they love it. In the USA, the North American Network of Women Runners (NANWR) has described the significance of jogging for women: 'Running out of the kitchen' is their slogan. 'We are saying a loud "No!" to subordinating our own needs, a daily run, to everyone else's.' Committing oneself to a martial art is a similar act of self-assertion, and many women report how once they take up any form of sport or exercise, the self-confidence and strength they achieve extends to all other areas of their lives.

Martial arts and other sports disciplines also have much in common as contributions to women's self-defence. Women runners often organize to run together for safety, as country tracks can be a combat zone. A 1981 NANWR survey of women marathoners found that 72% of the runners had experienced annoying comments, heckling, or harassment, two out of five had been threatened by a man or men, and 5% had been assaulted. Rapists are sometimes joggers themselves, or at least roam the paths in track suits; and women have put up signs on trees threatening the 'rapist-jogger'. Self-defence training can be invaluable for runners, and for any woman involved in an outdoor sport or activity like hiking, mountaineering, cycling or swimming.

At the same time, these sports themselves make a great contribution to women's safety by developing women's strength, confidence, and skills. Running is the first and most universal form of self-defence. In addition, we never know when our lives may depend on our ability to jump, climb, swim, cycle, throw, or just fight off exhaustion.

In reclaiming their bodies women are also reclaiming their right to enjoy any part of the environment, including the right to be in the countryside, to breathe real air and be in touch with nature, without the peace being eaten away by fear. It is an ongoing battle to be able to do this, and the same determination leads on the one hand to demands for safer streets and parks, safe, accessible training facilities, and better transport; and on the other hand to the massive enrolment of women in courses for self-defence.

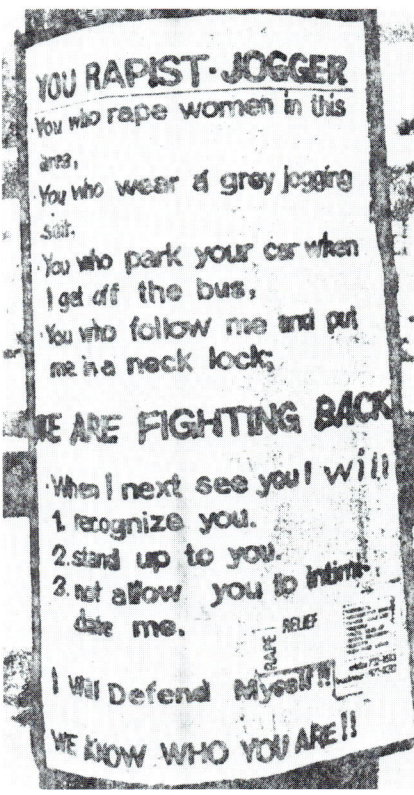

Above: *In New Brunswick, Canada, 1985, a Fredericton Rape Crisis Centre poster defends women's right to the streets and green spaces.*

Left: *Spending time in the countryside, away from city noise and dirt, and from other people, is important to many women. Too often such solitude and tranquillity are eaten away by fear.*

TAKING OUR TIME

For many women it is a struggle to gather the time, energy, and money demanded by serious physical training. In some places women are insisting on the resources to make fitness programmes accessible to all. In Philadelphia, for instance, a Women's Fitness Club organized by Phoebe Jones, Director of NANWR, offers childcare, a very low membership fee, and quality training for women at every level of fitness. In Britain some sports centres have a weekly women's day where childcare is provided. Childcare, free or at nominal cost, is a breakthrough; without it, most mothers of young children are excluded.

The cost of training is equally important. Most martial arts training, and many short courses in self-defence, are simply beyond the means of thousands of women, who therefore have less chance of defending themselves than women who are better off. And in any case, many women ask why they should be forced to pay for learning to deal with a problem in which they are the injured party. Many girls are now saying that self-defence should be taught for free, in school.

The provision of training in schools, colleges and workplaces, and the provision of childcare during classes, are all ways of tackling the obstacle of women's lack of time. Phoebe Jones writes:

> The minimum amount of time needed to achieve a beneficial aerobic effect is estimated to be between one and a quarter to three hours a week. This does not include the time involved in stretching or building muscular strength. Nor does it include showering, changing, traveling to and from a place of exercise, taking care of childcare arrangements, re-applying makeup, fixing hair, etc., which could easily double the time involved.

Above: *Many women like to have the support and comradeship of their own sex when learning the skills of self-defence.*

Women are now struggling to find or create courses with a *kind* of training suited to their needs. Many prefer women-only classes, not always easy to find, particularly for those who want a high level of training: women's programmes have always been under-resourced. Others prefer mixed-sex training, and increasing numbers of women enter classes previously catering only for men, and have insisted on the right to take part in all aspects of competition. Many have found male instructors and students helpful, and shared commitment to the art can build a rare mutual respect.

Yet the traditional power relations between men and women can prevail. Instructors may not explore what women can do best. Some women say that because they cannot make as big a commitment as men can, they are taken less seriously. Women who demonstrate superior skills may evoke hostility. Yet by their determination to make martial arts their own, women broaden them, to everyone's advantage.

In pursuing their own defence, by any means appropriate and necessary, in the home, in the streets, in waged work, and in the courts, women encounter every barrier to justice for themselves, and on an international level are pressing hard to knock these barriers down.

CHAPTER THREE

·HOW·TO· ·FIGHT·BACK·

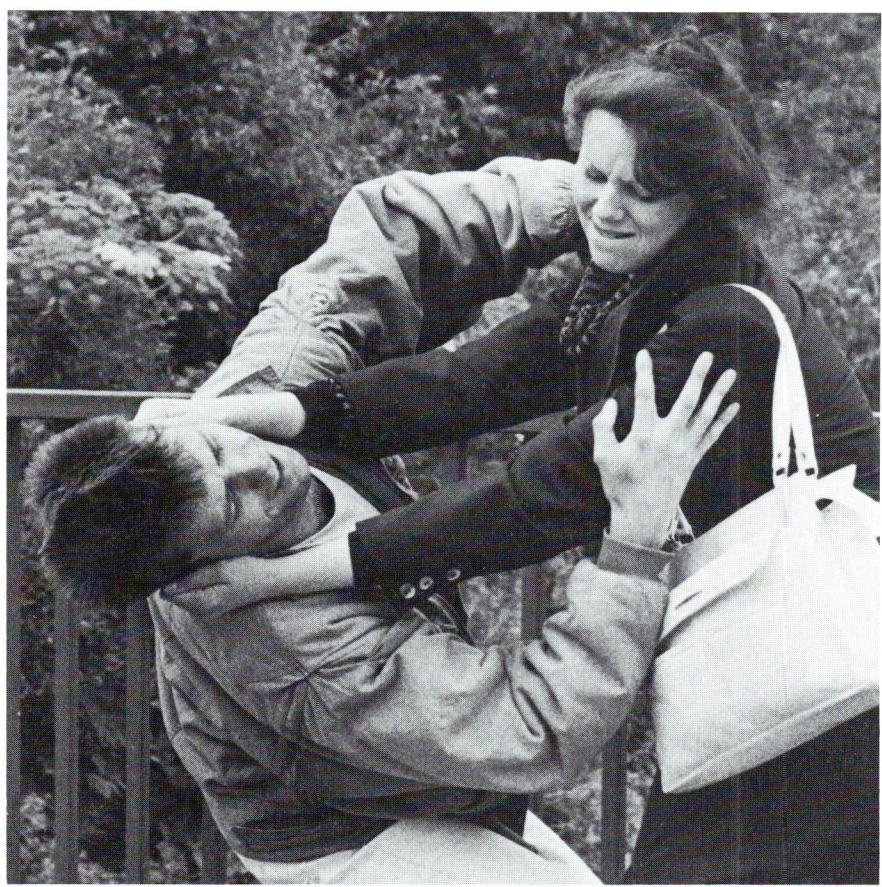

MANY OF THE TECHNIQUES SHOWN IN THIS CHAPTER have been taken from the Oriental martial arts and adapted so that they are practical for women's self-defence. All of the techniques have been thoroughly tried and tested, and particular emphasis has been placed on the ability of a weaker or smaller person to defend herself when confronted by a stronger attacker.

The striking and kicking techniques have been derived from karate, a method of fighting with bare hands and feet developed in Okinawa from about 1609, and used by the inhabitants to defend themselves against the Japanese who had successfully invaded the country. The Japanese were generally heavily armed, while the Okinawans had been forbidden to carry any weapons by their invaders. The art was studied in secret until it was eventually taken to Japan early this century and then became available to the public, gradually developing into the styles practised today.

Various self-defence concepts have been incorporated from tai chi chuan, another striking art, but one which integrates the defender's inner potential energy. This was practised by the Chinese from approximately AD 520, and is still used by the older Chinese as a form of exercise and meditation.

The locks are derived from aikido, an art which uses an attacker's momentum and energy and turns them against him; it also places emphasis on harmonizing with the attacker. The throws are based on those used in judo, a method of unbalancing the opponent.

All of these martial arts have been carefully analysed and those techniques which are considered to be most effective have been incorporated, together with elements based on street-fighting, army combat and common sense to produce the demonstrations shown in this book. Particular emphasis is placed on avoidance rather than direct conflict of strength. The methods described should provide the reader with a number of practical self-defence moves which are easy to learn and will either incapacitate an attacker completely, or give the potential victim enough time to make an effective escape. A few techniques which are a little more complicated are also included for the interest of those women who already know something about self-defence.

As it is impossible to forecast how an assailant will carry out an attack, many situations have been used in the demonstrations with a variety of people of various ages and sizes. Indeed, the only thing you can be certain of in self-defence is that no assailant is likely to attack in the same way as another. You do not require a large number of techniques to defend yourself, and you will probably want to select those that suit you best. But whatever you do decide on must be executed as if your life depends on it — perhaps it does.

AVOIDING DANGER

If you can avoid a potentially dangerous situation, then do so. Most attacks can be avoided; the problem is finding out how to minimize risks without becoming paranoid. It is most sensible to use the techniques described here only when there is no alternative.

When walking along a road, stay on the side with the oncoming cars travelling towards you, then nobody can unexpectedly proposition you, or even worse, pull you into the car. Walk on the outer third of the pavement so that you can see into dark doorways and gateways to make sure there is no one lurking there. If the street is deserted and traffic-free, walk right down the middle.

Try to avoid dangerous areas like gloomy lanes and short cuts through woods. If you must walk in a deserted or lonely area, keep alert to possible attacks: listen for footsteps, watch the shadows; better still, take a large dog with you.

If you think someone may be following you down the street, cross over. Take the opportunity of quickly looking at the person and assess whether he looks a bit suspicious and how far away he is from you. If he crosses too, then cross again. If he is really following you, he will also have to cross once more and you will now have time to consider what to do. You may feel confident enough to out-run him to the nearest well-lit, busy place; do so. If you reckon he will out-run you, then keep an even pace but lengthen your stride. If you obviously start to walk faster, this may well precipitate an attack, because the potential assailant will realize you have become aware of him. With luck there may be a public telephone nearby; go straight to it and dial for help immediately — you are not being foolish. Trust your instincts. If there are lights in someone's windows, walk up to the door and ring the bell. If the man starts to run after you and you need help quickly, bang on the nearest door and yell 'Fire!' as loudly as you can. This will bring an immediate response because people will want to see what is going on and whether their own property is at risk. Their nosiness will be sufficient to scare off your attacker. Shouting 'Help!' may not bring any response at all because, unfortunately, many people simply do not wish to be involved in others' troubles, especially in large cities. Alternatively, if you carry a personal alarm, let it off. The more noise you make, the better. This should be enough to get rid of him.

Most muggers look for an easy victim, a person who seems defenceless and weak. So if you look and sound confident you stand more chance in a confrontation. If you are the passive type, practise running; this may be your best method of avoiding trouble.

All too often, muggers strike in broad daylight, even when there are other people around. They rely on surprise and may do something to distract your attention, such as ask you the time, or may rush at you and trip you up so they can grab at your bag or jewellery while you are off balance. When visiting certain cities — Rome is especially notorious — travel agents will advise you not to wear valuable dangling earrings or necklaces which can easily be ripped off you. Apart from their loss, you may also suffer considerable physical damage. Be alert to possible attack whenever you are on the street, so that you are less likely to be taken by surprise. A shoulder bag with a thick strap, worn diagonally across the body and over one shoulder, with the flap on the inside, is far more difficult to snatch than a clutch bag. It also leaves your hands free to defend yourself if need be. A money belt is well worth considering.

If someone asks the time, stand well back, look the person in the eye and say 'Nearly three' (or whatever the approximate time is). If you feel at all doubtful about the character, it is better not to look at your watch, because you can easily be mugged while you are off guard. Similarly, if someone asks for directions, again look him straight in the eye and say 'Keep walking straight ahead and turn left at the traffic lights' (or whatever is appropriate) without turning round yourself and pointing out the way. As before, this can leave you momentarily off guard and susceptible to an attack.

Old or disabled people often feel particularly vulnerable to assault, as do pregnant women, but there is still a great deal they can do to defend themselves. Shouting aggressively can be enough to put off a potential assailant, who will not wish to have any attention attracted to himself. It needs very little strength to jab an attacker at the base of the throat with a finger, or scratch at his eyes — both highly effective techniques which can be used in dangerous situations and are discussed later in this chapter. If you know you can do something to help yourself, this will give you confidence.

MUGGERS AND PICKPOCKETS

Above: *A handbag worn across the chest like this is difficult to snatch. If the flap is next to the body, then your wallet will be safe, too.*

THE ELDERLY OR DISABLED

PUBLIC TRANSPORT

When travelling on a train, even if it is not late at night, try to select a carriage with other people in it, or even better get into the carriage with the guard. Sit near the emergency handle in case of need — and don't be afraid to use it. If there is a gang of rowdy youths on the train, get into another carriage at the next stop. Ensure that you are not followed into an empty carriage by a suspicious character, and if you are, get out quickly.

If you are on a bus and sense that some man is taking an unreasonable interest in you and that he might try to get off at your stop and follow you home, you can always stand up at an earlier stop and see if he stands up too. At the last minute, sit down again and see whether he does the same. If he does, you may well have reason to be worried and you can then tell the ticket collector or driver. Many bus crews are now in radio contact with the police. You can encourage them to ask the man which stop he wants and make sure he gets off there. Alternatively, get off at a busy place where you know he will be unable to molest you, and where you can find help.

THE TECHNIQUES

If you are ever forced to put up a fight, don't make half-hearted attempts which will often only aggravate an attacker. Every move must be executed forcefully, using every ounce of your strength to make each strike tell. If you worry about hurting your hands or feet as you strike, your punches and kicks will not work because you will hold them back.

You must strike wholeheartedly without worrying about injuring your attacker. If you are not prepared to do this, you must either give in or run away. If a technique misses its target, follow up immediately with another.

However, you should avoid direct conflict with your attacker's strength. Rather than blocking his attacks directly, try to deflect his movement or else side-step. Then hit your assailant as he is moving forward, thereby adding his momentum to your own, and you may disable him before he can start another attack.

Anything you are carrying can be used as a weapon to defend yourself. Use your imagination and analyse the potential weapons you have with you, to work out how you would use them for self-defence. A heavy handbag can stun an attacker if hurled at his head. Keys can be used to scratch at the face or eyes. A rolled newspaper or magazine can be wielded to make a strike at the groin, or the end can be jabbed under the nose. A shopping bag thrown at an attacker will surprise him and may allow you to escape. A coat wrapped around the forearm can protect that arm and could help you to block a knife attack.

THE LAW

Remember, however, that if you live in a place governed by English law, any seemingly innocent object can be construed to be an offensive weapon if used to injure someone — even in self-defence. In principle, the defence must not be disproportionate to the force of the attack. So if a man grabs you and you manage to jab him in the eye with your keys and blind him, then you could well find youself facing the charge of assault causing grievous bodily harm. In certain States of America, however, the law is not so strict. Find out what your rights are from your local police.

WARMING UP

Although several effective techniques, such as finger jabs to the throat or eyes, take little strength or muscular effort, others require a certain amount of flexibility and are more physically demanding. You may suddenly find that you need muscles you don't normally use, especially where kicks are concerned. It is best, therefore, to warm up first, before practising with a punchbag or partner, so as not to run the risk of pulling anything. If you already attend a keep-fit class or if you go jogging, then so much the better.

Start slowly, especially if you are not used to physical exercise. The body should be moved gently initially. Start at the head and work down; this way you will be less likely to leave something out. If any of these exercises cause discomfort, then don't do them. What is suitable for one person, may be inappropriate for another. If you have any physical problem then check with your doctor and ensure that he or she is happy that you can start exercising, and find out what range of movements can safely be performed.

The repetitions recommended here are based on the average person's fitness level and may need to be adjusted to suit your own ability and age.

LOOSENESS

1 Rotate the head slowly and in large circles to loosen the neck muscles. First drop the chin to the front, then move the head to the right. Then round to the back, chin raised, rotating to the left and back to the front again. Keep the shoulders down and stay relaxed.

Repeat about five times first to the right, then to the left.

2 Shrug the shoulders in a circular motion, first forwards, then backwards, for approximately 10 times each. If you have stiff shoulders, take extra time on this exercise, and repeat the rotation of the joints for a little longer than recommended, until they move more easily.

3 While facing forwards, rotate the hips in a circle, first pushing them to the front, then to the right, round to the back, to the left and forward to the front again. Always keep the shoulders still.

Repeat 10 times to the right and then to the left, or until the hips feel nice and loose.

4 Bend the knees, and place the hands just above them on the lower thighs. Move the knees in small circles, taking care never to force the joints or straighten the legs.

Circle the knees about 10 times, first to the right, then to the left.

5 Lift the big toes, while keeping the other toes on the floor, and push the knees in. Then lift the other toes, with the big toes on the floor, and push the knees out. This exercise helps with the positioning of the foot for the kicks shown in the following section, as well as improving coordination.

Repeat 10 times each.

6 Slide one hand down the leg as far as possible, then change over to the other side. Make sure that your body does not tilt forwards or backwards.

Repeat five times each side.

7 Place your legs apart, but keep them still and move your upper body from the waist in a large circle. First bend down to the front, keeping your neck loose, then raise your arms and upper body to the right side. Bend backwards as you rotate, then round to the left and down to the front again, stretching out as far as possible. Stop if you get dizzy.

Repeat for five complete circles, first to the right, then to the left.

8 Very slowly drop your head to the right knee, bending from the waist rather than the small of the back. Do not force the movement if you find it difficult; just relax into it. Repeat to the left.

Perform this exercise about five times on each side.

To perform the kicks you are at a distinct advantage if you are flexible, because this will allow you to kick to a higher target if necessary. Generally, however, the lower targets are more practical. Practise so that you can easily reach the attacker's groin or knee with your striking leg.

Always stretch very slowly, without any abrupt movements, and never continue if you are in pain.

STRETCHING

1 Spread your legs wide, but in a comfortable position, with your feet parallel and toes to the front. Keep one leg straight and lean slightly over this, but 'sit' on the other. Place one hand just above the bent knee joint on the thigh and push your thigh towards the floor, pulling your weight backwards over the bent leg as you proceed.

Repeat five times each side.

2 Sit on the floor with your legs as far apart as possible. Reach forwards and attempt to put your head on the ground, bending from the waist rather than the middle of the back. Relax into the position and hold it for the count of 30. Each time you breathe out, try to bend a little further forward. If you find this exercise easy, then try to put your chest and stomach flat on the floor.

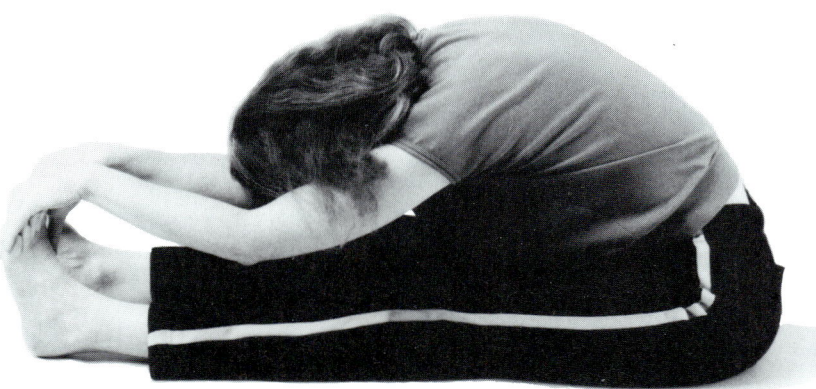

3 Sit on the floor with your legs slightly apart. Breathe out and stretch forward until your hands reach your toes. If you can manage this, then grab hold of your feet and pull your toes gently towards your head to stretch the hamstrings.

Hold for a count of 30.

4 Find a partner, someone whom you can trust to assist you. Keeping your back straight, place your foot on your friend's shoulder. She may have to bend her knees initially. Push your foot hard in a downward direction on to her shoulder, ensuring that your leg is always held straight. Count to 15. As soon as the count is reached, relax, then allow the partner to push your leg gently upwards while you hold the stretched position again for the count of 10. You will find, with this method, that your ability to stretch will gradually increase. Repeat with the other leg.

STRENGTH

Press-ups can be performed in several ways and should be tailored to suit individual needs. Start with the simplest method and progress to the more demanding as your arms, shoulders and back develop power.

The simplest press-up is performed with the hands flat on the ground, immediately below the shoulders, and the knees bent and resting on the floor, slightly apart. The back is kept straight, with the bottom tucked in. Repeat about 10 times.

Once you are able to do 10 press-ups from a kneeling position, straighten your legs and repeat a further 10 times. Build up to approximately 30 repetitions. When you have achieved this number without stopping, your arms will be really strong. You can now move on to the press-ups performed on the knuckles, as described in caption 1.

The next stage is to develop power in the finger tips, instead of using flat hands: repeat the press-ups with only the finger tips on the floor. This is particularly useful for performing the claw hand technique.

1 A more advanced press-up is performed with the two punching knuckles and the tips of the toes only touching the floor. This should be repeated as many times as possible, and will build powerful punches. (It should be noted that children should not be allowed to perform knuckle press-ups, as they may deform their hands; the bones are not sufficiently hardened until they are fully grown.)

2 Lie on your back, while your partner stands between your chest and your biceps facing your feet. Hold her legs tightly and lift your legs until she can hold your ankles in her hands. She then pushes your legs to the floor; you should allow your legs to lower, but not to touch the floor. When they have lowered to just about six inches (15cm) from the ground, start to lift your legs back towards her hands for the next repetition.

Repeat 10 times. An excellent exercise for the stomach muscles.

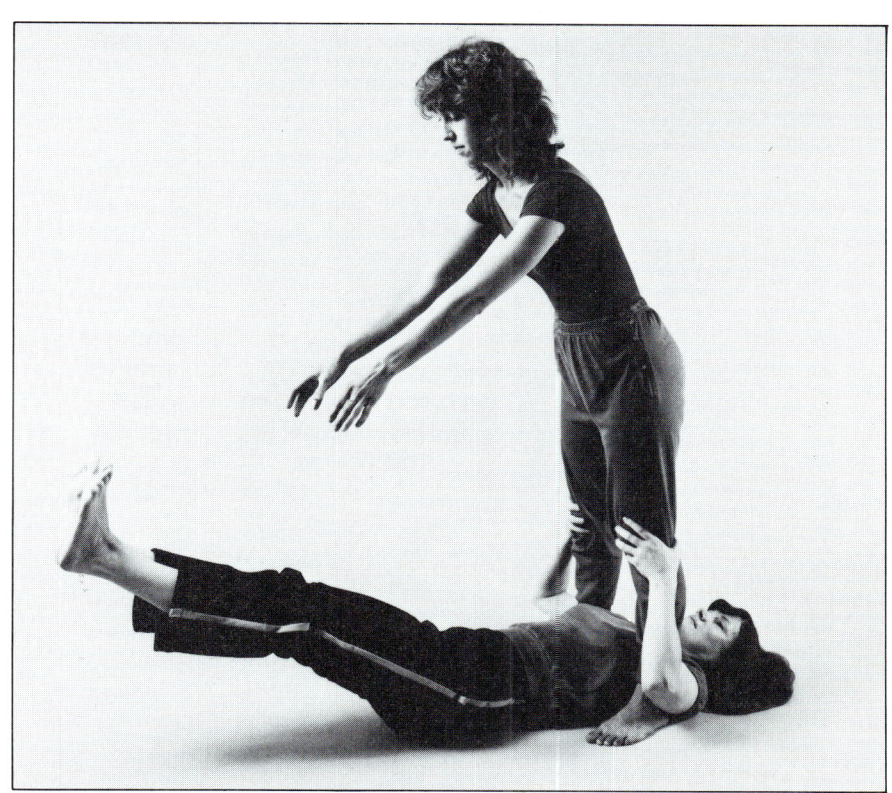

3 Sit back to back with your partner on the floor and link arms. Start with the legs straight out in front. Now draw the feet in to bend both your legs. Using the leg muscles, push hard against the floor, always maintaining an upward and backward pressure, and stand up together. Then sit down together by reversing the process.

Repeat about five times.

4 Sit on the floor facing your partner, with the soles of your feet touching, legs bent. Hold hands and, while your partner pulls backwards, try to stand up half way. Then sit down and support your partner while she tries to stand up. You should get a see-saw effect as one of you stands while the other sits and pulls.

Repeat about five times each side.

HAND TECHNIQUES

Any part of the hand can be used to strike an opponent, provided sufficient power is behind the attack, but there are some ways of holding your hand which will minimize the chance of injuring yourself, forming an effective weapon that will cause some real damage to anyone who is attacking you.

The use of hand strikes as opposed to kicking techniques will ensure that you remain fairly well balanced while defending. They are more appropriate for use by the older person, who may be rather unstable while standing on one leg.

Whenever an attacking movement is made, it must be performed with full power and a feeling of confidence. If you are at all unsure of a move, don't use it. All attacks must utilize the full body weight of the defender. If it is a straight punch the hips should be pushed forward into the attack. If it is a circular strike, the hips are twisted around and thus reinforce the striking hand.

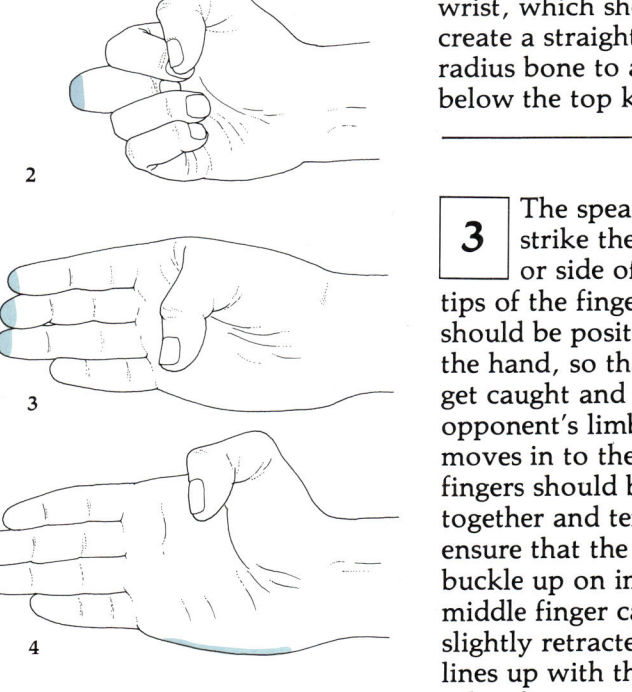

1 The front fist is used to hit the head and chest. The fingers should be tightly clenched, with the thumb folded out of the way on the outside of the hand across the first two fingers. The impact area constitutes the two knuckles and first bones of the index and second finger. Notice the correct alignment of the wrist, which should be used to create a straight line from the radius bone to a position just below the top knuckles.

2 The one-knuckle fist is used to attack the throat and solar plexus. The hand forms a very similar shape to the front fist, but with the second knuckle pushed forward and used as the contact area. It should be aimed at a soft target, not a large bony area, as the knuckle may buckle in if used on, say, the chest.

3 The spear hand is used to strike the stomach, throat or side of the ribs with the tips of the fingers. The thumb should be positioned across the hand, so that it will not get caught and break on the opponent's limbs as the hand moves in to the target. The fingers should be held tightly together and tensed; this will ensure that the hand does not buckle up on impact. The middle finger can also be slightly retracted, so that its tip lines up with the tips of the other fingers.

4 The outer edge of the hand, known as knife hand, is used to strike the side of the neck, groin or floating ribs. The fingers are held tightly together, with the top of the thumb pushed into the side of the hand. This strike travels towards its target in a chopping movement, and hits the opponent with the side of the palm below the little finger.

None of these techniques can be learnt and remembered merely by reading a book. They should be practised many times over until they become a conditioned reflex. It is preferable to practise with other people, who will keep you going even when you are getting bored or tired. The movements must be practised even when you feel you 'know' what to do, and they should be repeated again and again at regular intervals, to ensure that they are still at the back of your mind and that they can be called on when required, without hesitation and without having to think about them.

If you can obtain access to a punch-bag, or any of the equipment used to train boxers, then do practise on it. If none of the more conventional training aids is available, improvise with something else; hitting an old mattress or pillow is far better than punching at thin air.

The hand positions shown here are taken from karate and have, through trial and error, been developed over many years.

5 The thumb side of the hand is used to strike the groin, side of the neck or floating ribs. The formation of the hand is exactly the same as the preceding technique, and the base of the forefinger is used as the striking area. This is generally referred to as ridge hand.

6 A claw hand is used to catch the eyes and scratch the face. If you have long fingernails you will find that you will be unable to make a correct fist; the remedy is therefore to change your defence to a claw hand, or cut your nails. It is executed in a downward movement and is particularly useful when the attack is vicious.

It is worth noting that the police may well find the skin under the nails particularly useful when investigating the crime.

7 A bear hand is used to strike upwards under the chin, to jolt the attacker's head back sharply, causing either a whiplash injury to the neck or a throw to the floor, which can result in unconsciousness should the attacker hit his head on the ground on landing. This hand position may also be used to strike upwards under the nose, or into the solar plexus or groin, depending on the position of the defender.

8 A hammer fist is used to strike at the back of the neck or at an attacker's body if he is standing at the side of his intended victim. The striking area is the side of the hand next to the little finger.

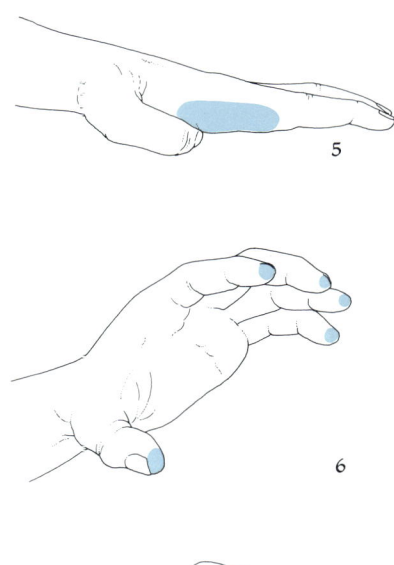
5

6

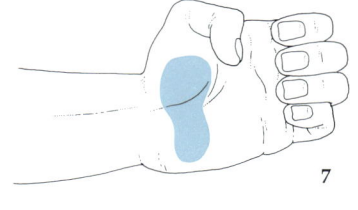
7

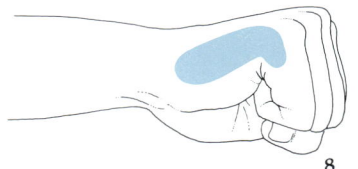
8

Remember that a soft target like the throat is most effectively damaged by a small striking area, such as one knuckle, the finger tips or side of the hand. A larger target area such as the head or solar plexus needs a powerful fist punch to cause any real damage.

Although the hand positions described here are the ideal forms to use, other positions of the hand invented on the spur of the moment will probably work, but may cause some injury to the bones. In a self-defence situation, anything is better than nothing. Don't worry about spraining a wrist or breaking a finger joint if your life is at stake; the hand will recover, but you may not.

HOW TO PUNCH

Form a front fist as described on page 64, caption 1. The basic karate punch starts by the waist, fingers uppermost. The fist must then travel in a straight line to its target. At the last moment, just as the arm straightens, twist the fist over and propel it into the target. The two main arm positions are demonstrated by the girl punching in picture 2. Further impetus is added by twisting the hip into the punch and by breathing out on impact. Always keep the shoulders down. Good balance is provided by bending the front knee. On impact, the back leg straightens, driving the punch through the target.

Get your partner to hold a pillow in front of her, and hit this as hard as you can. Imagine you are punching right through the pillow, not just at the surface. If she moves back or complains, then you know your punch has power. You will find that as your punches improve, your partner will have to use several telephone books for protection.

A simple and cheap item, a tennis ball, can be used to assist with target practice. Pass a piece of string through the ball and tie a knot in one end. Pin the other end of the string to a door frame, so that it can swing easily. Now punch at the ball; practise striking the ball as it swings towards or away from you. If you can hit this small moving target, you are doing very well.

Look at your opponent's eyes, not at the hands, but at the same time be aware of everything his or her body is doing. As a right-hand punch comes towards you, prepare yourself by quickly raising your left fist up by your ear then, with your arm bent at a right-angle, drive it downwards and forwards to sweep aside the oncoming punch with the point just below the wrist.

If you step to the side at the same time, your attacker will keep moving forwards and you are then in a good position to counter-attack with a punch to the head using your right fist.

An open-hand block can be made in a similar fashion and the palm of the hand can be used to sweep aside an on-coming punch or kick, rather than the bony area below the wrist.

HOW TO BLOCK

1 A practical method for practising targeting, coordination, blocking and punching requires the assistance of a partner. Stand with the left leg forward and punch towards your partner's face. As the punch arrives she should block it across her head in a deflecting movement, using an open-handed block. Once she has blocked your punch, she pulls her blocking hand back and punches towards your face with her right fist and you now perform the block with your left hand. Provided each of you has your left leg forward, the order is punch with the right, block with the left. As you begin to get the feel of the movement, start to speed up and see how fast you can punch and block. Repeat with the other foot forward, using the opposite hands.

2 If you can find a large ball similar to a football in size, then get another friend to hold this behind your partner's head. Punch the ball, but make sure that you miss your partner's head and hit the ball as hard as possible. Ask the person holding the ball if the punch would have worked; as she is on the receiving end of the strike, she is in the best position to assess the amount of power generated by the punch.

KICKS

The martial arts use a variety of kicking techniques, but many are extremely complicated and take years of practice to perfect. In a self-defence situation the kicks must be: a) easy to learn; b) easy to execute; c) effective; d) the best weapon for the target. Given these restrictions there are three types of kicks which will work. These are the low front, the side and back kicks.

LOW FRONT KICK

The first kick to learn and the easiest is the low front. This kick has two forms: one with the instep straight and the toes curled under; the other with the instep bent and the toes raised. The position of the foot in each case is shown in the drawings below, together with the relevant attacking area.

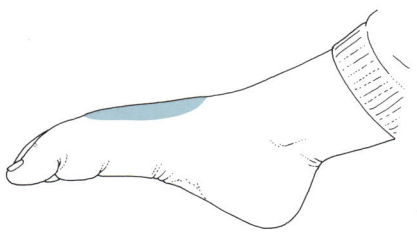

1 The first method, with the instep straight, is used when attacking the groin. This ensures that, even if the kick is slightly off target, some part of the foot will contact the groin area. If the foot does contact completely on target, an extremely painful and debilitating response will result.

2 The second form of the front kick, with the instep bent, can be used when the defender's ankle movement is restricted. This could be caused by the potential victim wearing high-heeled boots, or possibly, in the case of the elderly, suffering from stiff ankles. This form of kick is also used when attacking a hard, but sensitive place such as the shin bone. Since the striking area is the ball of the foot, an area accustomed to pressure, this will not be damaged when the kick lands.

The movement of the leg is the same in both cases.

HOW TO KICK

First of all make sure that the foot is not taken behind the body line, as this movement will telegraph your intentions to such an extent that your target will probably move before your foot is anywhere near it. Simply raise the knee to a height which allows the lower leg unrestricted movement, as shown in the drawing on the left.

Once the knee has been raised, the lower part of the leg flicks towards its target. The faster the leg moves, the more damage it will cause. Don't worry if you are not strong; the speed of the kick will make up for it. If you thrust your hips forward at the same time, more weight will go into the kick and it will be even more effective. The position of the leg, as the foot strikes, is demonstrated in the first photograph on page 70.

Withdraw the foot instantly so that there is no chance that your assailant will catch it.

Left: *Put your hands on your hips when practising a front kick to ensure that they are thrust forward into the attack.*

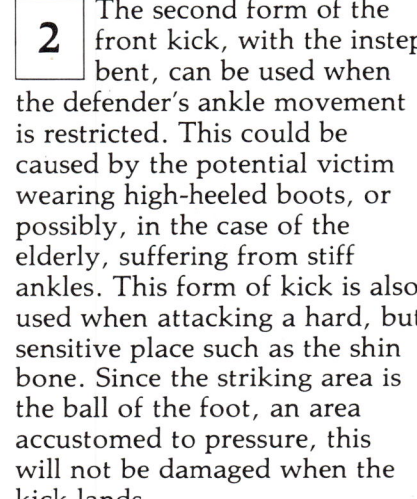

SIDE KICK

The edge of the foot is thrust out when your opponent is standing at your side.

It is best employed for an attack to the stomach, knees, shin and foot. A kick to the knee will incapacitate an attacker, and allow you time to run away, or take other evasive action.

The shin is struck when a 'diversion' is needed to allow other defences to take place. It causes pain, but does very little damage. It is useful in getting rid of a pest, someone whom you would prefer to deter rather than injure or maim. When using the shin attack, hit the shin just below the knee with the edge of your foot and keep pushing downwards, keeping contact all the time: you should scrape all the way down the shin bone, forcefully landing on the instep with the side of your shoe.

The foot is usefully attacked only if you are wearing high heels and can stamp downwards with all your weight into the instep. If you are wearing soft shoes, forget it. You will probably annoy the assailant even further, causing yourself yet more problems.

The knee is lifted in the same way as the front kick and then, with a twisting action of the hip, pushed, very strongly, sideways and downwards towards the opponent, becoming in effect a stamp. The side of the foot must land on its target with all of the body weight behind it, or a loss of balance, due to recoil, may result on impact.

A similar type of recoil occurs when a rifle is fired, and always occurs when hitting a hard object very forcefully.

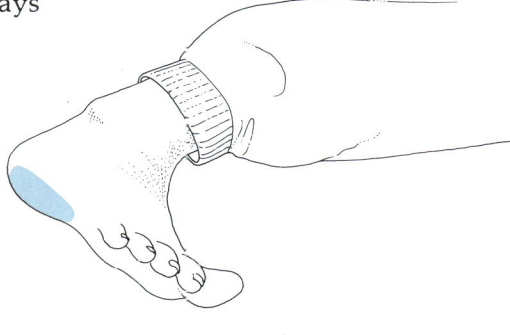

BACK KICK

If you are attacked from the rear and your arms are trapped, you may have to resort to the back kick. The execution of this technique can be difficult as you do not necessarily know where your opponent's legs are. The easiest target to find is the foot. Apply a very heavy stamp, but remember, only use this kick as an opening move and immediately follow with a stronger attack to ensure that you can get away, or at least leave your assailant in a position where he can cause you no further trouble.

The heel provides a good weapon for a strong back stamp on to your assailant's foot. Alternatively, the outside edge of your foot can attack the shin. As in the other kicks, lift your knee high first, then thrust the foot sharply backwards and down, tensing it on impact.

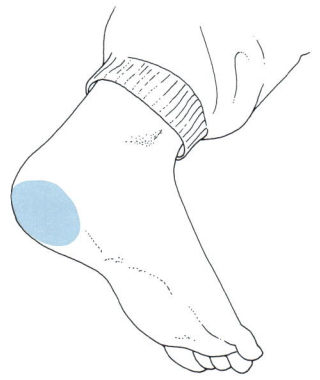

PRACTISING KICKS

The front and side kicks should be practised with the assistance of your partner. Persuade her to hold a pillow or a similar soft item in front of her as a target. The kicks should be practised as many times as is possible, to ensure that the movements are 'programmed into the subconscious' and will occur automatically when they are required. Always ask your partner's opinion of the technique, and then take heed of her remarks. If she says the kick has no power, then try to improve on the speed, power and movements you are performing.

1 This is the front kick in which the toes are raised and the weapon is the ball of the foot.

2 In the side thrust kick, the foot is flexed and the outer edge is used as the weapon. The impetus is provided by the hip which swivels into the attack as the leg straightens.

At a lower level, the edge of the foot can be aimed at the knee, or scraped down the shin.

3 One way of practising the front kick involves a partner. Hold hands and kick towards your partner's hip, first one side then the other. Don't kick to the centre of your partner, but towards the left then the right hip, alternating sides with each kick. As you kick, your partner should move the side of the hip that is being kicked backwards with a twisting motion, while keeping the body completely upright. This allows your partner to practise deflecting movements. If you ever find yourself moving away from a strike too late to avoid it completely, the power of the attack can be reduced by twisting the body in the direction of the kick or punch, thus deflecting its power. As you become more confident, speed up.

The knee can be used to great effect, especially if your assailant is very close — a situation which can be difficult to escape from, as the closer a person is to you, the more strength it requires to push him away. The knee can quickly come between you and your opponent and from an angle which is quite unexpected, below the line of vision.

As long as you put all your weight behind the knee as you lift it, it can be used to attack the groin or solar plexus very effectively.

The knee can also be used to strike the opponent's head. It is very difficult even for a martial arts expert to reach an attacker's head if he is standing, and impossible for most people, so you will have to bring the head to you. Pull it on to your knee by clasping your hands around the back of his head or shoulders, or by grabbing his ears or hair and wrenching the head down sharply.

This is a strong technique and has more 'impact power' than the kicks.

This is because the knee is closer to the centre of the body, and can be powered in with the full body weight behind it, by pushing the hips forward or upwards. As long as it is used on low targets, it is one of the best natural weapons. The knee attack is further illustrated in the graveyard sequence later in the chapter.

THE KNEE

The elbow strike can be used to attack any vulnerable area. It is a very powerful weapon and is most effective when your attacker is close.

There are two areas which can be used to strike with, either along the forearm or the upper arm. The point of the elbow is not recommended here as this can cause damage to the defender's elbow joint. The forearm is turned, so that the thumb is facing towards the defender's chest, and swung into the movement, using the hips as a fulcrum. When the upper arm is used, it is reinforced by dropping the hips downwards.

A further application of an elbow strike is discussed and demonstrated in the sequence set in the graveyard later in the chapter. In this practice picture, the defender is facing her opponent with one leg forward; she uses a hip twist to swing the opposite arm into the attack. In the graveyard sequence, the woman uses the momentum created by the assailant to swing forward with the same arm and foot.

THE ELBOW

A swift elbow strike to the chest can easily wind an assailant. To begin with, the arm must be held well back, elbow bent, with the fist just above the waist, fingers uppermost. Step into the attack and swing the elbow forwards, meanwhile bringing the forearm across the chest and turning the fist downwards. Strike with the bone of the forearm.

VULNERABLE POINTS

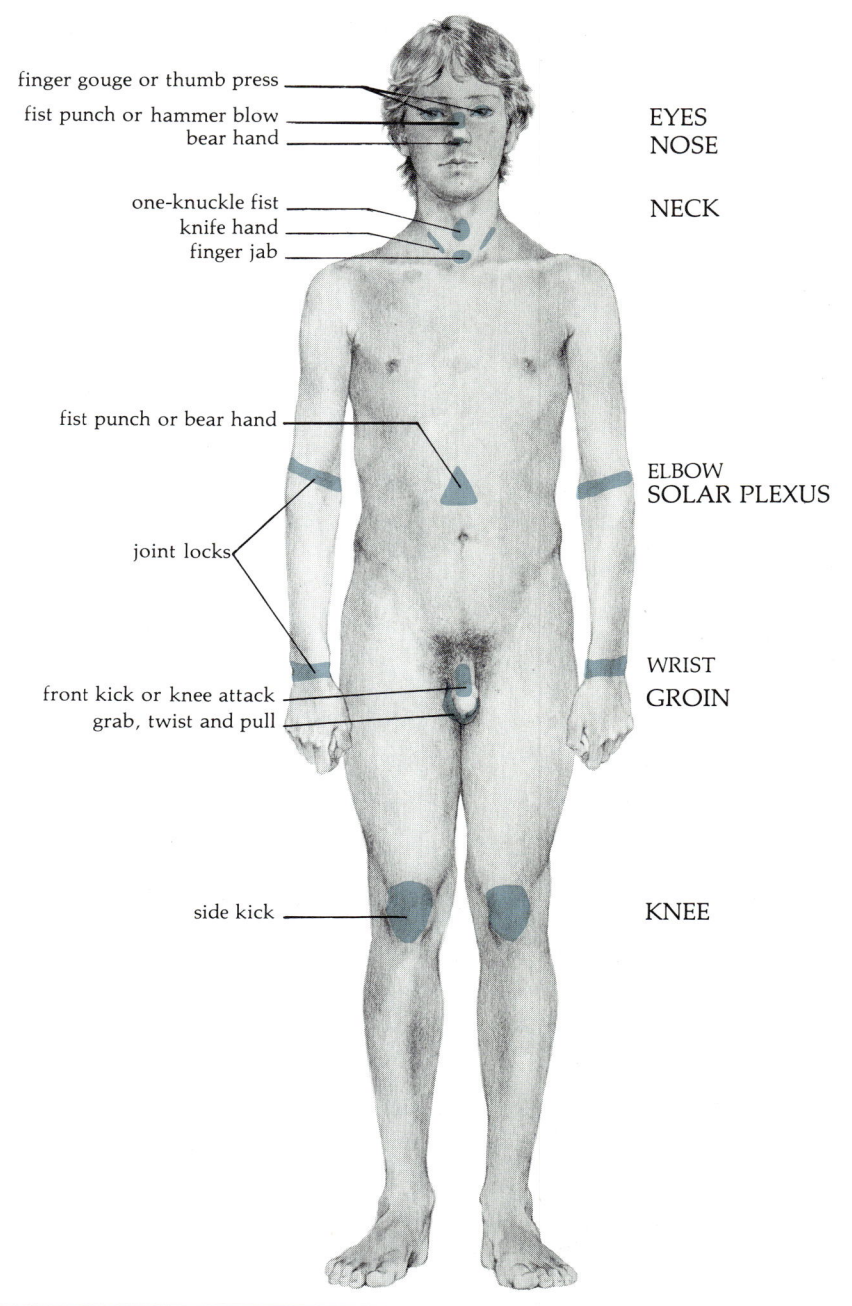

finger gouge or thumb press ——————

fist punch or hammer blow ——————

bear hand ——————

EYES
NOSE

one-knuckle fist ——————

knife hand ——————

finger jab ——————

NECK

fist punch or bear hand ——————

joint locks

ELBOW
SOLAR PLEXUS

front kick or knee attack ——————

grab, twist and pull ——————

WRIST
GROIN

side kick ——————

KNEE

KIAI!

Whenever you strike at a target, you should kiai. A kiai is a loud shout, which comes from the pit of the stomach. It is used to give courage to the defender, reinforce the strike and to startle the attacker. Try to imagine that your stomach has, very suddenly, been pushed in, and expel all of the air from your lungs. As you strike, shout 'eeeh' at the time of impact.

Weightlifters use a similar method when lifting a very heavy weight, to enable them to concentrate their energy at the moment of the lift.

Many women have convinced themselves that as the 'weaker sex', they stand no chance in a physical confrontation. This is just not true. Many women are actually stronger than some men. The main problem when a woman is being attacked is her tendency to panic and freeze, thereby creating a situation where she is unable to defend herself even if she is physically very powerful and under normal circumstances quite capable of looking after herself. To avoid the freeze-up situation, or the other less common response of flailing about and generally aggravating the attacker, it is absolutely vital to remain calm.

One of the many ways of learning to remain calm and still use all your power is to practise ki exercises. *Ki* is a Japanese term which loosely translated means 'potential energy'. The exercises which are shown within this book will help you learn to use this powerful energy.

It is estimated that the average human uses only one-tenth of his or her potential energy, and that the other nine-tenths are used only in cases of dire stress. There has been a case of a woman lifting a car, when her child was trapped underneath; of people caught in a fire carrying valuables which they could not formerly lift — the list is endless.

This type of energy, although very powerful, can go out of control, and unless it can be contained within a calm mind, is very dangerous. You do not want to maim a passer-by simply because he asked the time, and you misconstrued his intentions through panic.

The real secret of this potential energy lies in the mind, not the muscle. If you believe you can do something, then you can do it.

When you punch at a real target, imagine it is not actually there, that it is like a shadow or a cloud. This is the only way that you can be absolutely sure that you are punching with all your potential energy.

When punching or kicking a target, try to hit right through it, aiming for the wall or the ground behind it — depending on where it is positioned. You will be amazed at the force you can generate.

All of these exercises are performed with a partner, preferably someone at least as strong as yourself, so that you can then be sure you are using your ki energy.

POTENTIAL ENERGY

KI EXERCISES

STAYING CALM

1 Stand in front of your partner just out of arm's reach. Ask her to punch towards your face and look at the fist as it comes towards you. Don't cringe or shut your eyes.

APPLICATION

To ensure that you keep calm in the face of danger, and can work out what you are trying to avoid.

UNBENDABLE ARM

2a Bend your right arm slightly. Ask your partner to press down on your upper arm with her left hand and grasp your wrist with her right, pushing with all her strength to try to bend your arm some more. Resist as much as you can by using the force of your muscles. If your partner is stronger, then he (or she) will bend your arm quite easily. If less strong, then feel in your muscles how much forceful energy you have to put into your arm to prevent your partner from bending it.

2b Try again, but this time imagine that your arm is made of iron and that nothing can possibly bend it. Don't tense your arm and fight your partner's strength with your strength as you did the first time, but rather overcome your opponent's strength solely with your concentrated mind. If you concentrate on the iron arm firmly enough, you will find that your partner will be unable to bend it however much she may try.

Children are particularly good at this exercise. They have more vivid imaginations than adults and can visualize more easily.

APPLICATION

However big or strong your assailant might be, you need not worry — just use your ki energy and concentrate on your defence.

3 Your partner is going to lift you from the floor. Her hands should be placed under your armpits, to give a vertical lift, without tilting you backwards. Again, this exercise is in two sections. The first time imagine that you are as light as a large balloon and are flying upwards to the sky. This kind of lift should be very easy.

Try again, but this time imagine that your feet are glued to the floor. If your feet come up, so does the floor. Don't tell your partner which one you are practising; let her tell you.

UNMOVABLE PERSON

APPLICATION

If your assailant is trying to lift you from the floor, keep calm and visualize strongly that you are glued to the ground, and there is a good chance that he will be unable to move you.

AWARENESS

4 Ask your partner to stand behind you, and very slowly punch towards either of your shoulder blades. The punches, although slow, should be performed with maximum intent. Try to guess which shoulder is being attacked. Don't look round; just try to guess. As you practise, you should find your guesses becoming more and more accurate.

APPLICATION

Most attacks come from the rear. Once you can detect a person approaching you from behind, you stand a much better chance of taking evasive action.

INNER POWER

5 Find a partner who is, preferably, larger than yourself. Put your hand on her chest and push. She should try to remain still. The first time use your strength, push as hard as you can and see how far she moves.

On the second attempt try to reach the wall with your push, ignoring the fact that your partner is there. Compare the distance that she has moved this time with your first effort.

APPLICATION

To ensure that you are not hitting just the surface of a person, but punching straight through him.

PRACTISING TECHNIQUES

The descriptions in this book are not intended to imply that you have to have a certain leg forward, or are only of any use if the attack is exactly the same as that shown in the picture sequences. All of the moves can be used from the right and the left sides, and it should be assumed that the techniques are available to both left- and right-handed people.

Find a partner who is, preferably, stronger than yourself and work out the most suitable moves for your build and temperament. It is necessary to practise from both left and right stances and be prepared for an attack from any direction. It is also just possible that one of your arms may be injured, either by your attacker or through some previous misfortune, so practise each technique with both left and right hands. Once you have learnt to perform the technique from the given direction, try it with the other foot forward and use the other hand. Then ask your partner to attack you from the other side.

There are, therefore, four basic positions to practise the moves from: *a)* attacker in left stance (i.e. left foot forward), defender in left; *b)* attacker in left stance, defender in right; *c)* attacker in right stance, defender in left; *d)* attacker in right stance, defender in right. Find as many as possible directions and angles from which the technique can be performed, and practise all of these, as well as the ones listed.

Work out which is your best target: if you are short you may not be able to hit the head, and if you are very tall the attacker's groin may be too low. Perfect the techniques which come to you most naturally, then you will know for sure that you can rely on them in an emergency.

When confronted by an amorous stranger or even more likely a 'friend' with whom you have some previous acquaintance, who believes that you cannot possibly find his advances unattractive, it is necessary to make your intentions absolutely clear.

NUISANCES

If you are seated, move somewhere else. Don't run away, or appear panicky; try to ignore any comments he may make. If it is obvious that he is still persisting, it is very important to tell him that you are not at all interested in a very firm manner. Don't sound apologetic, as he may interpret this as a 'come on'.

If this does not deter him and he starts 'groping', try to ensure that the situation does not become worse. If you are in a location with other people around speak very loudly; his embarrassment at being shown up in front of other people may well be enough to reduce his ardour. A loud comment such as 'Get your hands off me' will probably work.

If even this fails, it may be necessary to cause the man a certain amount of pain, to ensure that you have enough time to get out of the way. The technique shown in the photographs will not injure the assailant but will certainly give him something else to think about. It is not advisable to use this technique if the assailant is anything other than bothersome. A violent or serious attacker would require a much stronger and incapacitating response.

ONE-KNUCKLE DEFENCE

1 In the photograph shown here the girl is obviously not interested in her admirer, but is aware of him.

2 As he closes in she draws away. She lifts the hand furthest away from him as he starts to touch her knee, then forms a fist ready for a one-knuckle strike. (See under Hand Techniques.)

3 Using all her power she strikes the back of his hand with her second knuckle, leaning her upper body forward and down into the strike to ensure that her full body weight is behind her fist.

BULLIES

There is a definite point in a relationship when it is time to say no, and mean no. If this statement is not made and actively reinforced, it allows a bully to carry on his dubious activities. After all a bully is only a bully when the going is easy; if it looks as if it might turn into a struggle he is generally not interested.

In the sequence shown here we are dealing with a bully. The girl obviously knows the man because she has allowed him to come so close. In this particular situation it is quite likely that she has been bothered by him before and has now decided to make a stand. If she does not know the man the response should be completely different and she should run away.

DEFENCE WITH A BOOK

REMEMBER

Ordinary objects can make excellent weapons. But keep within the law and make sure that any force you apply is justifiable in the situation.

1 As she is carrying a book, it is appropriate that she should use it. It would be foolhardy to drop the book, which, considering her size, is one of her most valuable weapons. The man grabs her shoulder and pulls her towards him.

2 She keeps hold of the book as she is pulled forward. She is not resisting the pull as she is going to turn the forward motion to her advantage and actually steps towards the man. She must ensure that at no time does she lose her balance. This may seem to be an obvious statement, but most people who are being attacked panic so much that they are incapable of keeping their feet underneath themselves, and may fall to the ground. She must breathe deeply, therefore, and stay calm. Meanwhile, she grasps the book at the corners with both hands, and swings her arms back slightly.

3 She then steps forward and strikes at the attacker's solar plexus with the corner of the book, using a forward and upward motion, keeping the arms straight all the time.

In the sequence shown here we are again dealing with a bully: a boy who needs to be deterred rather than pacified. The girl perhaps knows the boy and feels she can deal with him. However, in a more dangerous situation, for instance if the attacker is unknown to her and has a weapon, she would be well advised to give him the bag without hesitation — she can always get another.

The third step in the sequence is optional, depending on the amount of force considered necessary in the situation.

1 The bully grabs for the bag, but the girl is determined that he will not get it.

2 She takes a step with her right leg towards her left leg to adjust the distance, and to ensure that she remains

SHIN SCRAPE

balanced while she executes the following side kick. She lifts her left leg, raising the knee high, and in a stamping motion drives her weight downwards on to his shin. (NB If this were a more serious attack she would aim at the knee.) The foot is positioned with the side of the heel leading into the target, and all her weight behind the kicking foot. The boy reacts by dropping his head and body down — leaving him open to a follow-up kick.

3 The girl drops her left leg to the ground and, ensuring that she is well positioned for the next kick, twists her hips sharply to the left kicking his chest with her shin and instep. The 90-degree turn of the hips is necessary when using this kick, as it allows the full weight of the body to be driven into the target and makes the kick sufficiently powerful to cause some damage.

If this were a serious attack the target would be the groin, and the weapon the instep driven upwards by a powerful front kick.

It is important to remember your height and build, and know what you are capable of. If you are shorter than your attacker, you should only hit what you can easily reach; don't attempt to hit somebody's head if it could in any way affect your balance. Hit a part of the attacker's body which is well within your range.

SEDUCERS

If you do not want somebody's attention, make it absolutely clear. A woman may try to repel an admirer in a weak, ladylike voice. The man then becomes very confused regarding her intentions. Is she really interested? The tone of her voice indicates that she might be, but the words say something else. You cannot expect an admirer to read your mind. He may misinterpret body language signals, or a tone in the voice, and get the wrong impression of your real intentions or desires.

If you go to a party 'dressed for the kill', you can also expect to attract admirers as you walk home. If you are alone, it is advisable to put on an overcoat if you wish to be left in peace.

GROUND DEFENCE

Although the man in the photo sequence is only being a nuisance, the situation could very easily develop into something rather nasty.

1 The girl, has, unfortunately, decided to sun-bathe in a solitary spot. As she is rubbing sun-tan cream on her legs, the man has assumed that she is encouraging him. She had no such intentions, but he thinks she is sending out 'I'm available' signals. He approaches, but she still hasn't realized he is there, and that he is interested in her.

2 As he caresses her, she barely pulls away, nor does she make any negative statement. No doubt she has been taken by surprise, but her lack of reaction is likely to be misconstrued. He pushes her to the ground, now so engrossed in her that any negative response would probably be ignored and taken as a 'come on'.

3 Once on the ground, she decides that she must act. She is really leaving it rather late, and would not have had to resort to such actions if she had repelled him earlier. She thrusts his head back with a claw hand, and pushes against his groin with the other hand.

4 She forces him over. His interest in her has suddenly disappeared. She should consider herself very fortunate.

If you are sitting or lying on the ground and see signs of a potential attacker, keep your eyes discreetly on him, but don't under any circumstances appear to be encouraging him. If he comes too close and leans over to make a grab at you, keep your feet between him and the rest of your body, with your weight on one side. This leaves one leg free to perform a few well-placed kicks.

ALTERNATIVE GROUND DEFENCE

This picture shows the woman hitting her assailant's knee with the heel of her shoe.

You can practise with a partner, but, obviously, kick gently. The knee is a tender target.

SEATED DEFENCE

When in a seated position, it is far more difficult to execute a self-defence move. The strike cannot be reinforced with a hip movement which provides the impetus for the technique. This sequence demonstrates the body movements required to generate force, and shows a method of utilizing the attacker's reactions to obtain additional impact.

1 The man in this sequence is interested in the girl. After sizing her up, he slides along the bench towards her.

2 He puts his arm around her shoulder and pulls her in tight. She draws back and tells him to let her go, but he ignores her request and tightens his grip.

3 Afraid for her safety, she twists from the waist and swings back the arm nearest to him across her chest, raising her elbow so she is ready to strike.

4 Then she hits him in the chest with an elbow strike, which forces his body forwards.

5 As his head is lowering, she lifts her fist and strikes at his nostrils, which makes his eyes water. She should make sure that her elbow does not move once the chest strike has been performed. If she does move it she may signal her second strike and give him the opportunity to counter.

Once he has been temporarily blinded she should make good her escape.

DRUNKS

A drunk is very difficult to deal with, as he may have a high pain threshold and so cannot feel anything. He may not be able to rationalize, so that you can tell him to clear off repeatedly without getting any response. In fact he is probably not even listening, and even if he were he would not understand what you were saying. If you push him away he may get angry. A drunk's actions are unpredictable so you cannot guess what he will do next.

Look for signs of drink: a slurred voice, a red face, the smell of alcohol. Stay out of the way, cross the road, run — do anything possible to avoid a drunk. He will always have an excuse for his actions and blame his appalling behaviour on the alcohol. Afterwards he may well claim to remember nothing of a particular incident.

The girl in this sequence is being bothered by a drunk. She doesn't particularly want to injure him, just to cause enough pain to allow her the time she requires to run away. A drunk may well find it difficult to pursue someone. Often enough he cannot even walk in a straight line.

WRIST LOCK

1 The girl is enjoying the view and does not see the drunk approaching.

2 He starts being friendly, puts his arm round her shoulders, and pulls her towards him. Detecting the smell of alcohol, she decides to get rid of him quickly.

3 She reaches across and pins his hand to her shoulder. Still holding it there, she moves backwards and turns underneath his arm.

4 Now she has grabbed his hand with both of hers, and twists his wrist.

5 She holds his fingers out straight with her right hand, and, rotating in a downward direction, she forces him backwards until he starts to lose his balance, as he tries to avoid the pain.

6 As soon as he is on the ground she makes a run for it.

FRONT HAIR GRAB

This sequence shows a drunk grabbing at a passer-by's hair. She has to act quickly and with full intent as she has no idea why he has taken such action.

Whenever an attacker pins part of your body, keep that part still and defend yourself with a free limb. Here the head is pinned, and the girl cannot pull it free from his grip, so she uses her hands instead.

  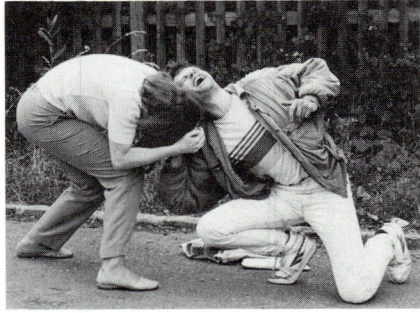

1 The drunk seems to be ignoring her and the girl has every reason to suppose that he will walk straight past her.

2 He makes an unsuspected grab at her hair. Immediately she drops everything she is carrying and pins his hand to her head, taking care that his hand is tightly covered with both of hers. She cannot pull away, as she will either drag him with her, or lose some of her hair.

3 She takes a large step backwards, keeping his hand on her head, and executes a lock by bending straight down. This forces his wrist backwards, bringing him to his knees to avoid the pain.

4 Once he is down, she lets go of the hand, and finishes him off with a kick to the ribs, before making her escape.

This sequence is a variation of the previous hair grab release, but is applied when the attacker approaches from the rear. Again, a wrist lock is used.

REAR HAIR GRAB

1 The drunk comes out of the pub and approaches the girl from behind.

2 He grips her hair and pulls her backwards. The girl is totally surprised, but manages to keep calm.

3 To remain balanced she takes a step backwards, towards him, keeping his hand pinned to her head. She takes the opportunity of stamping on his instep, as she twists under his arm.

4 Then she applies the lock by lifting her body. The hand, still pinned to her head, is twisted at the wrist and forced back.

If he hasn't already released his grip, then she is now in the ideal position to execute a groin kick.

SHOULDER GRAB

The principle of this defence is that if an attacker's head is forcibly moved, the remainder of the body will of necessity follow the direction of the head. It is a good way of forcing someone to the ground without hurting him unduly.

1 A girl is enjoying a stroll in the park, when a drunk lurches towards her. He stops to chat.

2 He grabs her shoulders to pull her in closer. She immediately lifts her hands between herself and his chest. She pretends to respond, but then grabs his ears with both her hands.

3 She twists his head sharply towards the ground, so that he starts falling sideways.

4 He lands on the footpath. The follow-up kick to the groin will not be necessary if it appears that he has no intentions of getting up.

The best self-defence techniques are always straightforward, but they do require the victim to have her wits about her and not to panic, especially if the situation is likely to turn nasty.

Be very careful when practising this attack to the eyes with a partner. It is best to do it in slow motion only, ensuring that the nails do not make contact. Better still, draw a man's head on a football and ask your partner to hold it at the correct height. Then it doesn't matter how vicious your counter-attack is.

POTENTIALLY DANGEROUS SITUATIONS

REAR ARMS GRAB

> ### REMEMBER
>
> If you sense that someone is following you, LOOK ROUND discreetly to assess the situation and be prepared to act quickly.

1 This girl has just been to the local shops and is walking home across a footbridge. She realizes that someone is behind her, but thinks nothing of it.

2 The next moment a man has grabbed her arms and is attempting to pin them behind her back. If she struggles to pull free, he may well tighten his grip and make it impossible for her to move her upper arms.

3 Instead, she twists her hips sideways as soon as she feels the attacker's grip, and before it has tightened. By turning, she is able to free one arm; she has taken the line of least resistance.

4 She uses the free arm to prepare for a strike, by straightening her fingers and bending her thumb out of the way. He still has one arm pinned.

5 By sweeping her hand in a rising arc, she attacks his eyes with her finger tips, grazing them from right to left. The scratching that results from such a defence is not seriously damaging, but it is sufficient to cause temporary blindness from profuse watering. The attacker will automatically slacken his grip and the girl can run away.

UPPERCUT AND WRIST LOCK

The woman shown in this sequence is using rather a complicated but effective wrist lock. It is inadvisable to try this technique unless you can first practise it properly and are confident that you can use it. If you have the opportunity of joining a good self-defence club, then make sure you try this technique out under supervision. Wrist locks are well worth mastering because they require relatively little strength and bring about total submission from your assailant.

REMEMBER

Tight clothes restrict movement and high heels throw you off balance. If you are walking in a lonely place it is prudent to wear a more practical outfit.

1 The girl has decided to take a short cut home, but she is startled by a man who has been waiting for her behind a wall.

2 He runs towards her and grabs her shoulders in an attempt to pull her down. The obvious defence at this point would be a sharp front kick to the groin, but unfortunately the girl's skirt is too tight.

3 She therefore swings her right arm down and executes a powerful uppercut by striking under his chin with a rising punch. His head jerks back.

4 His hand is still on her shoulder, so she pins it there with her right hand and grips the inside of his elbow with her left.

5 By twisting her hips 90 degrees away from him, she turns his hand so that the palm is facing up.

6 Keeping his palm up and pinned to her body, she swings back to face towards him, bending his arm into an S shape. She pushes his elbow down and applies pressure to his wrist by bowing towards him. The pain forces him to the ground.

7 Once he has fallen backwards, she kicks the side of his knee cap with her heel. She has dealt very ably with her attacker: he has a broken or sprained wrist, together with an injured knee, possibly dislocated.

WRIST GRAB

1 If you are walking in a lonely place, be alert to signs of danger. In this sequence the woman has been taken by surprise: a man has grabbed her wrist. He pulls her towards him. She instinctively tries to escape by tugging her wrist away, but because he has a more powerful grip she has no chance of fighting him off with only the force of her muscles. The more she pulls away, the stronger the retaliatory response becomes.

2 She then changes her tactics and allows her attacker to pull her forward and, using his motion, she hits him sharply with her elbow. One way of creating the momentum required for this technique, is deliberately to tug the arm away, then as soon as you get a response, suddenly step strongly into the attack.

Note that the woman steps in with her left leg in order to strike with her left elbow.

THE ELBOW STRIKE

Practice for an elbow strike has already been demonstrated earlier in this chapter, but the most important thing to remember is that the hips should be swung sharply into the move. This will greatly increase the impact. As the hips are at the centre of the body, swinging them sharply will whip the attacking limb towards its target. This can be compared with a wheel: if the hub (hip) is spun, the rim (limb) rotates more quickly than when the rim alone is spun.

Another point to consider is the strength of a woman, which is generally less than that of a man. If you hit with the elbow only, you are probably moving less that a stone (6kg). If you swing your hips as well, you will move most of your body weight into the target.

3 The elbow strike has caused him to release his grip and lower his head, giving her the opportunity to grasp the back of his head. (She could have grasped his ears, but in the heat of the moment finding such small objects could be very difficult, and it may mean that his head would slip away.)

She pulls his head down, while lifting her knee into his face. If she can hit the nose he will be temporarily blinded, as any strike to the nose will cause the eyes to water considerably.

Steps 1 to 3 should be sufficient to dissuade the man from another assault. If you carry the defence any further a court of law may well consider you guilty of assault. For instance, in England you may use sufficient force to defend yourself, but once the attacker is subdued and is no longer attacking, you should discontinue the defence, as at this stage you will become the attacker.

THE LEGAL SITUATION

4 If the woman genuinely feels that the attacker might still persist, she could follow up with a double-fist strike to the back of his neck. In this technique, one fist is placed on top of the other so that the strength of both arms is employed. Strikes to the neck can, however, be very dangerous and should be used only if in real fear for one's life. Be careful when practising this with your partner.

5 Again, the inevitable downward motion of the attacker's head can be turned to advantage by meeting it with an upward strike. The technique here is a kick, using the inner edge of the instep under the chin.

If this were a real situation, it is possible that a court of law may find the number of defences excessive and that the woman was therefore guilty of bodily harm. Remember that the force used in any defence must be just sufficient to put an end to the attack.

GANGS

If you run into a rowdy gang it is prudent to avoid trouble and get out of the way. If you are forced to take action, it is better to have a go at the leader first. If you can disable him, the remainder of the gang will probably disappear without causing any further trouble. A gang has to have a leader, or it becomes a collection of individuals acting independently. If the leader is disabled, the remainder of the gang has no way of organizing itself. The individual members of the gang may well be cowards at heart, and may cause trouble only if they can rely on the protection of the other members.

This sequence demonstrates a typical multiple attack. When the men first approach the girl, neither of them particularly intend to assault her. But as each of them is egged on by the other, the whole situation gets out of hand.

1 The girl is walking over a bridge. A couple of youths decide it would be fun to annoy her, so they prevent her from walking any further by standing either side of her. They start getting over-friendly, and make rather nasty comments. Naturally, the girl feels very threatened.

2 One of them grabs her arm. She cannot pull free. The other man, encouraged by his friend's boldness, grips her other shoulder.

REMEMBER

Use whatever weapons you have free. If your arms are grabbed, then defend yourself with your feet.

3 The situation is getting out of hand, so she reacts decisively. First she kicks the stronger of the two men on the shin with a side kick. He falls to the ground.

4 She now turns to deal with the other youth and swings her handbag into his throat. He falls backwards, unlikely to trouble her for a while.

5 The other attacker is about to get up, but a heavy kick in the groin with her heel stops any further action. She can now walk quietly away.

DANGEROUS ATTACKS

Many really dangerous attacks not involving weapons are aimed at the woman's throat or face. Unfortunately it is all too easy for a man to strangle, choke or suffocate someone with less strength than himself. However, remember that he is probably using both hands leaving parts of his own body unprotected, especially the groin. Counter-attack instantly with whatever weapon you have free and apply it with all your force.

STRANGLES

If you ever find yourself in the unfortunate position shown in the first photograph, try to keep your chin tucked in. This will temporarily prevent the strangle from taking effect. There are two basic types of strangle: the first blocks off the air supply by compressing the wind pipe; the second blocks the blood supply to the brain and is caused by pressure to the arteries in the neck. If you can tense your neck muscles and lower your chin the strangle will not take effect so quickly.

When being strangled you must react immediately. If you leave it too long, you will start to pass out. Allow a friend to take hold of your throat, but tell her to be very careful to ensure that too much pressure is not applied. This will give you practice in tensing your neck muscles and lowering the chin in a completely safe situation. The only way to avoid a panic if the real thing should ever happen, is to practise over and over again until the movement becomes a reaction. This will mean that the response will be performed automatically and you will not have to think about it.

GROUND STRANGLE

1 The woman in the photograph has tensed her neck and is ready to counter-attack. She has clenched her fists and is about to strike with the second knuckles; this technique is known as bear hand (see Hand Techniques).

2 She lifts her fists and strikes the floating ribs on each side of the attacker's chest with her knuckles. When punching in his manner, imagine that the opponent is not really there and attempt to hit your hands together.

As soon as the assailant loosens his grip due to the pain caused by the punches, she lifts one of her knees, ready for the follow-up.

3 She hits him very forcefully on the base of the spine with her knee, and simultaneously pushes with her arms, thus throwing him over the top of her head.

4 Once he lands on the ground, she acts quickly to finish him off. She forms a knife hand, commonly called a karate chop. In this technique the fingers should be tensed, straight and held tightly together. The thumb is bent, as illustrated earlier in the chapter. She strikes with the outer edge of her hand to the carotid artery, along the side of the neck.

Note that this is a dangerous technique, easily causing unconsciousness. When practising, stop the chop fractionally before it makes contact with the neck.

HEAD-LOCK RELEASE

This sequence shows a potentially very dangerous attack. The girl must act extremely quickly to ward it off. If she reacts slowly it may well be too late, and the assailant will be able to do whatever he likes with her.

In any defence the sooner you move the easier the defence becomes, mainly because the attacker is still moving towards you and can therefore be unbalanced, or, if you are well trained, can be manoeuvred on to your strike while you avoid his weapon, be it arm, leg or stick. Otherwise, as soon as he stops moving and grips you, you have to create motion from a stationary position, with the possible additional restriction of pinned arms or legs. Take, for example, a car: it is easy to push it if it is already moving, but as soon as it becomes stationary it requires a great effort to get it going.

1 A girl is enjoying a quiet walk down a lane, unaware that a man is surreptitiously approaching her from behind.

2 He grabs her round the neck and starts to pull her backwards. Being trained in self-defence, she immediately tucks her chin well in and grabs his arm to alleviate some of the pressure.

3 She pushes her hips back and to the side of his body. She is now in a position to grab his groin.

4 A quick twist causes him to slacken his grip around her neck.

5 Then she pulls. Remember the words: GRAB, TWIST AND PULL. Not many men will be able to continue an attack after such treatment.

AN ALTERNATIVE

1 If she is in a position where she cannot reach the groin to grab it, she has to change her defence.

2 She strikes the groin with the forearm. While she is executing this technique she imagines that she is aiming her hand at the sky. This is the only way she can ensure that the movement is executed with enough power to cause damage.

SEATED HEAD-LOCK DEFENCE

If the girl in this sequence were very alert, she might 'feel' the approach of her attacker and react much earlier, giving her the opportunity of taking evasive action, without the need for such a drastic defence.

Gouging of the eyes is extremely dangerous and can cause blindness. It should be used only to counter a severe attack when your life is threatened.

1 This girl knows her local country park well and has been here many times before. There are few other people around, but she does not anticipate any trouble and is absorbed in her book. She fails to notice a man approach her from behind.

2 He grabs her round the neck and tries to pull her backwards. She immediately pushes her chin down and grips his arm to take the pressure off her neck. Using her other hand, she grabs his hair, then pulls his head forward into range. (If the head is moved forcibly the remainder of the body usually follows.)

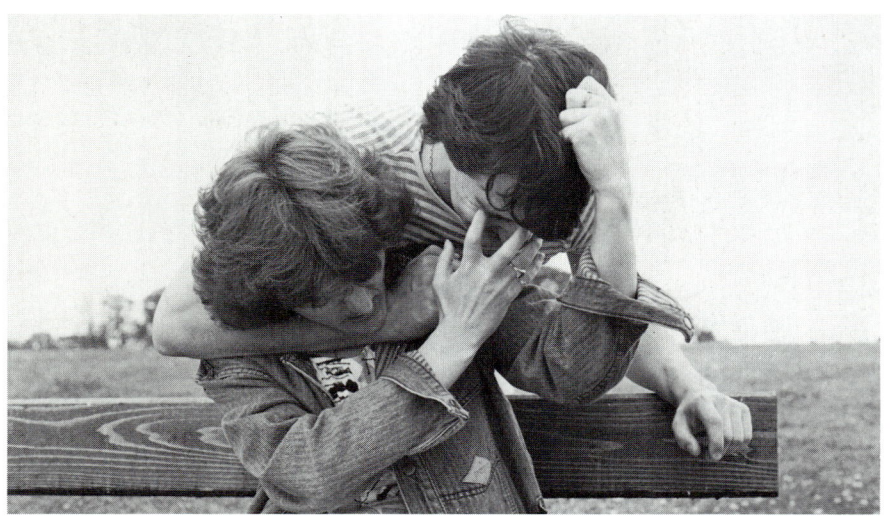

3 At the same time she makes a claw hand and pokes him in the eyes with sufficient force to cause temporary blindness so that he releases his grip and she can run away.

Practise this technique very carefully, in slow motion only.

When being grabbed around the throat, it is important to react instantaneously. You have only a few seconds in which to defend yourself.

Most of the frontal attacks to the throat take place with a support behind the victim, such as a wall, bed or floor. It is very difficult to strangle someone whose head and body can move, as they can usually step back out of range of the attacker's hands.

FRONT CHOKE

1 This sequence shows an older woman being attacked with such a strangle. As the attack starts she lifts her right hand ready for the defence.

2 She places her index finger into the pit of the youth's throat, just above the sternum, and, curling her finger slightly, pushes down and forwards. At the same time she grabs the groin.

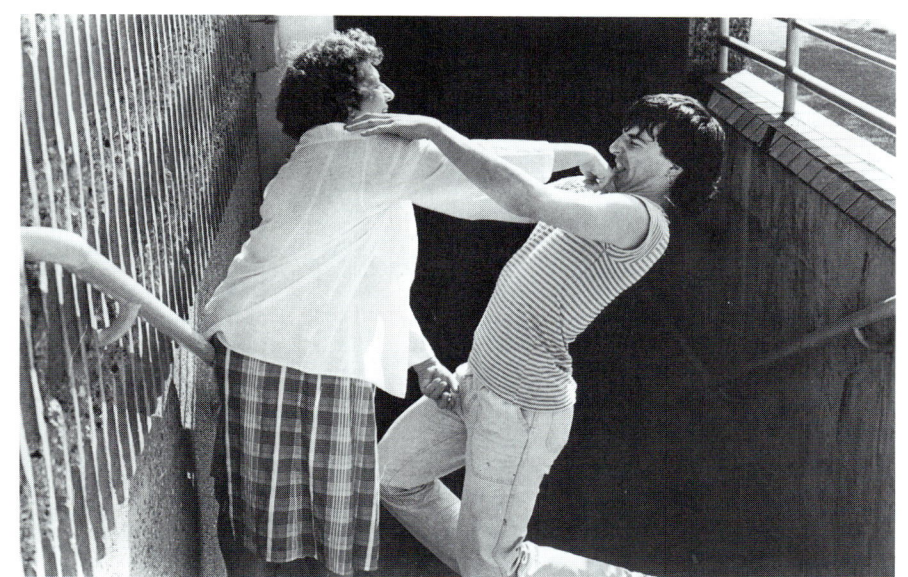

3 Using a levering action she pushes with her finger into the throat, and pulls the groin towards her. He will quickly release his grasp and fall towards the floor. She can then make her escape.

REMEMBER

Pressure into the pit of an attacker's throat requires very little strength and causes immense pain. This powerful weapon can be used effectively by the elderly or disabled.

REAR MOUTH GRAB

1 Dressed up for a night out, this girl had arranged to meet her boyfriend at the station, but he hasn't turned up. She telephones his mother to find out what has happened to him, not realizing that she has attracted unwanted attention.

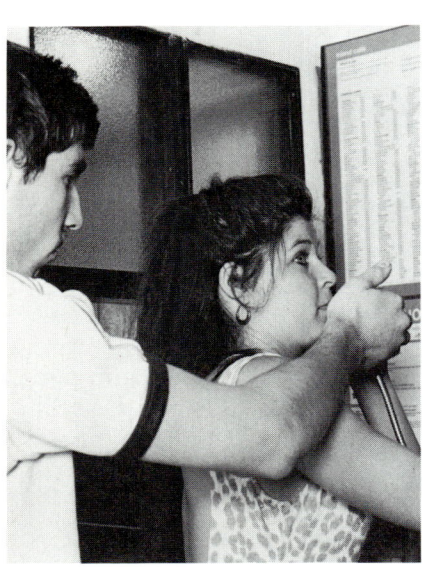

2 By the time she is aware of the attacker, her mouth is covered by his hand. She cannot talk her way out of the situation, nor can she run. She must react quickly. She holds tightly on to the telephone receiver, ready to use it as a weapon.

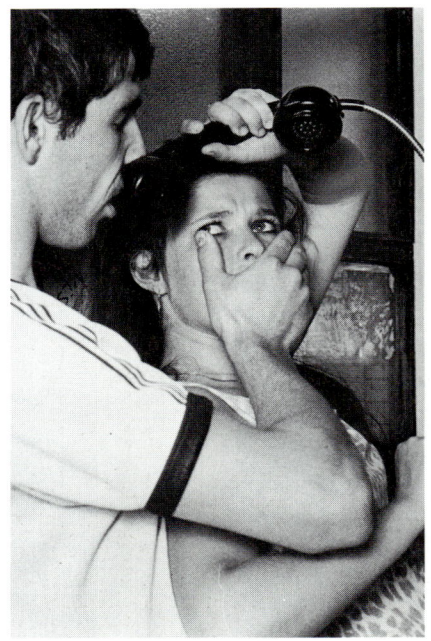

3 She lifts the receiver over her shoulder towards his face, and jabs him sharply on the nose. This causes his eyes to water and his grip to loosen.

4 Using the outside of her other hand, she quickly strikes him in the groin. He doubles up in pain and she can now run away. Alternatively, if his groin is within easy reach, she can grab, twist and pull.

MOTOR CARS

Unfortunately, motor vehicles have all too often been involved in crimes ranging from petty theft to rape and murder. By following a few sensible safety rules, you can enjoy driving around on your own and avoid the aggravation of burglary or the horror of assault.

If you leave your cameras and other valuables on the seats in full view, you should expect them to have disappeared on your return. You are inviting the robbers to help themselves and you may well end up with a large bill for broken windows and other damage to your car.

Before getting into your car, make sure there is nobody hiding in the back seats. Check your tyres and petrol before setting off and be sure of your route. Always carry any maps you may need and a torch. It is a good idea to belong to a motoring organization, so that you know someone will come to your assistance if you break down. Worry can be further reduced if you have a fully comprehensive insurance policy and a reliable burglar alarm.

When in a car keep all the doors locked, including the often-forgotten passenger doors. It is all too easy for someone to climb into your back seat while you are waiting at traffic lights. Should you need to ask directions, wind down the passenger window and shout across the car. If any problems arise the passer-by will not have time to reach you before you can drive away. Avoid picking up hitch-hikers. If the location is dangerous, keep the windows shut.

Should you find yourself inside a car with a man and the situation suddenly becomes threatening, start to retch and pretend you are going to be violently sick. He will have to let you out. There are not many men who will wish to have their precious vehicles ruined in such a manner!

It is far safer for a single girl to buy and sell her cars through a reputable dealer. If you display a 'For sale' notice with your telephone number, any would-be rapist can ask you for a test drive and take you to a lonely spot. A beautiful young Australian girl was raped and murdered not long ago when attempting to sell her Mini in just this way. If you must advertise in a newspaper, ask a male friend to accompany you when demonstrating the car to any potential buyers.

SELLING YOUR CAR

Left: *It is wise to be aware of possible dangers when getting into your car, especially in a lonely parking place. A door left casually ajar can be an invitation to a passing thief, as the sequence on the following page demonstrates.*

CAR THIEF

In the accompanying photo sequence, the girl uses her initiative by trapping the attacker's hand in her car door. The pain will cause him to withdraw it instantly.

1 This girl has climbed into her car, quite unaware of any trouble. If she had been a little more alert she might have noticed a suspicious character hanging around the car park. He creeps up from the rear of the car and avoids being seen.

2 He grips her shoulder in an attempt to drag her out of the car, threatening her with the knife. He demands the keys.

3 She quickly grabs the car door handle and slams the door on to his arm. If the motor is running she should drive away fast. Under no circumstances should she step out of the car and try to fend off the attacker. She stands more chance of escaping if she can drive away, or at least lock herself in.

If you are attacked with a weapon, do everything you can to talk your way out of the situation. Only attempt to defend yourself if you have absolutely no alternative, for instance when the assailant is about to stab you. Give up anything you are carrying or wearing, such as your handbag or jewellery. If you can run, then run. If he has a gun, then don't try to argue — do as you are told.

Unlike many other activities, self-defence has no rules; one assailant will not attack in the same manner as another. The person who is most cunning will stand the best chance of staying alive. In some situations you may be able to escape by throwing a fit or vomiting.

Anybody using a weapon is extremely dangerous, and you must therefore achieve a mental state of 'do or die' if you expect to be able to defend yourself. Half measures are worse than useless.

WEAPON ATTACKS

1 This woman has been surprised by a man threatening to hit her with a plank of wood. She tries to talk her way out of the situation, but without success.

PLANK ATTACK

2 As the attacker moves in, she steps towards him, thus putting herself too close to be hit. She blocks the wood with her left hand, while driving the heel of her right hand powerfully into his solar plexus to wind him. She must lean all her weight forward behind the striking hand, so that her body creates a straight line.

3 She brings her left foot towards her right, to enable her to get close enough for the following kick. She raises her front knee to allow her foot a direct line of travel towards the target. She kicks him firmly in the groin using her instep as the weapon. Now that he is incapacitated she can get away.

KNIFE ATTACKS

If you are approached by somebody carrying a knife and you are fast on your feet, then run, but if you are rather slow, it is better to be able to see what is happening rather than risk being stabbed in the back. A handful of sand or gravel thrown into his face will startle or temporarily blind your attacker and give you a head start.

If you cannot run away then try to use something you are carrying, or have picked up, to keep between yourself and the knife and use it as a shield. A large thick handbag will make a very good defensive tool if a knife attack comes towards your stomach. If you attempt to block the knife with your hands you may get your wrists cut, with devastating results. Use a coat to wrap around your lower arm and block with this.

If you are indoors, throw something through the window to attract attention and create as much noise as possible. A chair makes an ideal shield until, hopefully, help arrives. Always try to keep the central line of your body protected and never allow the knife near your stomach or head. You may well have some of your limbs cut, but as long as you can protect your vital organs, you should recover.

The sequence shown here is complicated, and should be learnt under expert supervision. If you can find a self-defence class, then join it. The techniques taught at the class may not be exactly the same, but they will deal with similar situations, and will give you varied practice at coping with an attacker.

CRESCENT KICK AND WRIST LOCK

1 In this sequence the woman has become suspicious of the man walking towards her. She stops as the knife appears in view, and tries to maintain a considerable distance between herself and the weapon. She thinks about running away, then realizes he could easily overtake her, so she decides to defend herself.

2 As his arm stretches forward, she kicks at his wrist using a crescent kick, making contact with the sole of her foot. Her shoe will give her some protection against the blade.

3 The kick moves in a semi-circular manner, forcing the knife away from her body. While he is off-balance, she immediately steps forward and grabs at his wrist.

4 Then, using both hands, she tightens his grasp on the knife. Ensuring that the blade is at all times facing towards her attacker, she starts to twist his wrist back on itself in a circular direction, executing a painful lock.

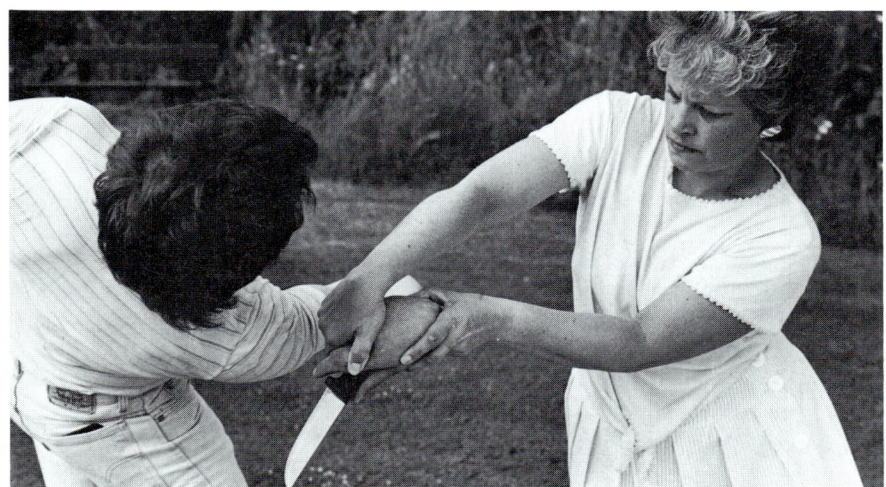

5 She takes a step back and moves her hips sharply to the left and at a right-angle to the attacker. She keeps turning her hips and twisting the wrist until he loses his balance. As he falls she follows him, maintaining the wrist lock.

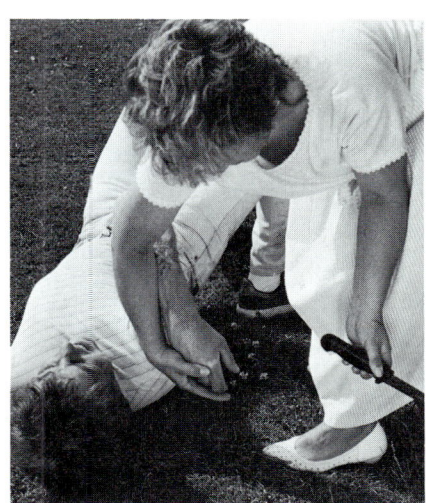

6 His hand automatically relaxes its grip on the knife, due to the pain in his wrist, and she quickly takes the weapon from his grasp. She now has the advantageous position.

TRUNCHEON ATTACK

The technique shown here is a figure-four arm lock and is applied to the elbow. It causes so much pain to the attacker that anything being held in his hand is dropped from his grasp. It can easily break the elbow, thus restricting any further attack. Despite this debilitating effect, the lock requires only a little strength to apply.

1 On her way back from the local swimming baths, this woman is grabbed from the rear by an armed assailant.

2 Reacting quickly, she drops everything she is carrying and hits up under his rib cage with an open-hand strike. He tilts forward, winded.

3 She grasps his wrist with her left hand and reinforces the grip with her right hand, by placing it under his arm.

4 She forces his hand backwards over his shoulder and applies an elbow lock by twisting and pressing down on his wrist with her left hand and pulling up under his elbow with her right. Although he has now let go of the weapon, she continues her movement until he falls to the ground.

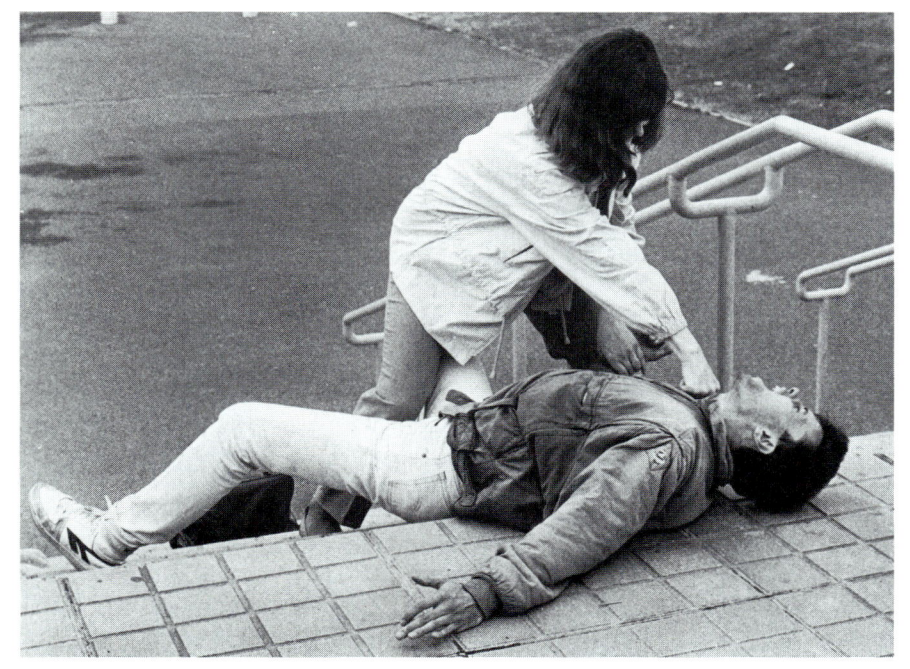

5 This finishing punch to the throat is reinforced by a downward push of the hips. This is a very dangerous technique and can kill. It should therefore be used only in extreme situations where the victim knows that she will be murdered by the man if he gets up. An alternative is to make the same punch to the solar plexus. If applied with sufficient force, it will wind the man long enough for the girl to run away and find help.

AT HOME

Provided that you take sufficient security measures it should be very difficult for a stranger to gain access to your home. Work out how you would get in if you had lost your keys. If you can find a way in, so can an intruder.

Window locks should be installed on every window, and a dead lock as well as a standard lock should be fitted to the front door. The police provide information leaflets to help you make your home secure — use them. Many communities have a crime watch group — find out about your local one and join it, then you can all keep an eye on each other's property.

Do not let strangers in! This may seem a stupid statement, but many people actually let an intruder in just because he claims to come from the telephone, gas or electricity company. Does he have an appointment? Do you know what his identification card should look like? If you are in doubt, don't open the door. Ring the company and check that they have sent somebody. Even better, refuse to see him until a proper appointment has been arranged.

If you come home and suspect that an intruder is inside, don't go in. Telephone the police from a neighbour's house.

THE TELEPHONE

It is best not to reveal your gender in the telephone directory if you want to avoid unwelcome calls. An initial rather than a complete forename is quite sufficient. There is always a chance that you might still be troubled by an obscene phone call and this can often be worrying. If the caller persists, you can soon put an end to his harassment by blowing a whistle loudly into the mouthpiece. An alternative is a resonant alarm clock.

Many people now have answering machines. If you have one, don't let it advertise your absence to potential thieves. Rather than saying on your message 'I am sorry I am out at the moment', say 'I am sorry I am too busy to take your call.'

Right: *Even if you are unlucky enough to be attacked while in bed, you can still defend yourself. A sharp jab under his nose with the heel of your palm will cause considerable pain and his eyes will water profusely.*

Far right: *Follow up quickly with a ridge hand strike to the side of his neck (see Hand Techniques). A blow to the carotid artery can cause unconsciousness.*

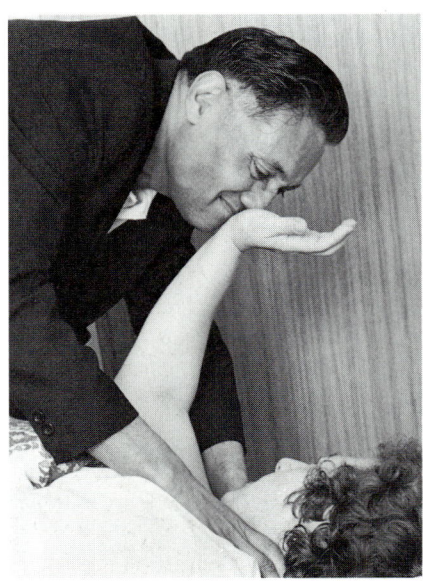
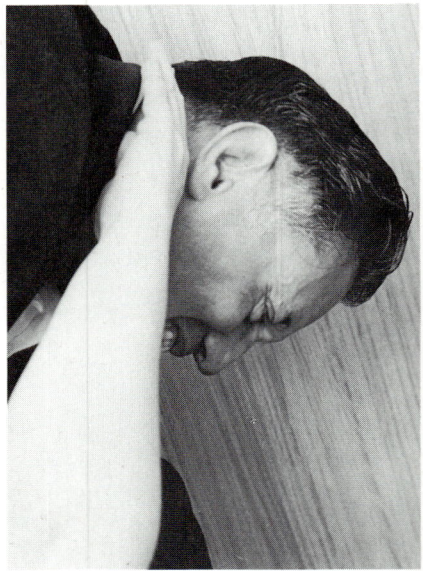

FRONT CHOKE RELEASE

1 An intruder has broken into the woman's house. She is quite unaware of his presence as she has become engrossed in a television programme.

2 As he grabs at her throat, she immediately lifts her right arm across her chest. Using the outer edge of her hand as a weapon, she strikes his ribs in an attempt to reduce the pressure to her neck.

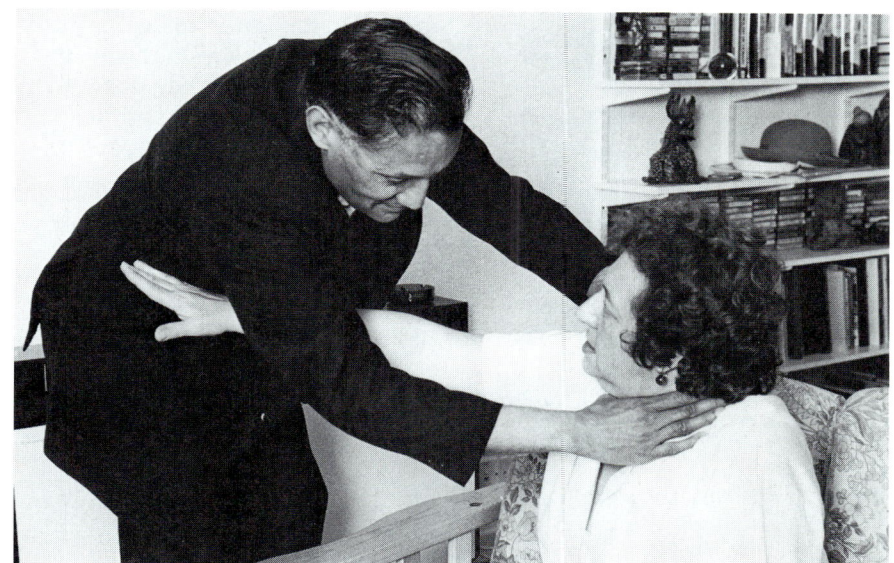

3 While he is still startled by the blow, she presses his eyes with her thumbs. She keeps pushing down until he release his grip. She should then run out of the house and call for help, or, if this is impossible, throw a chair or other large object through the window to attract attention and scream 'Fire!'

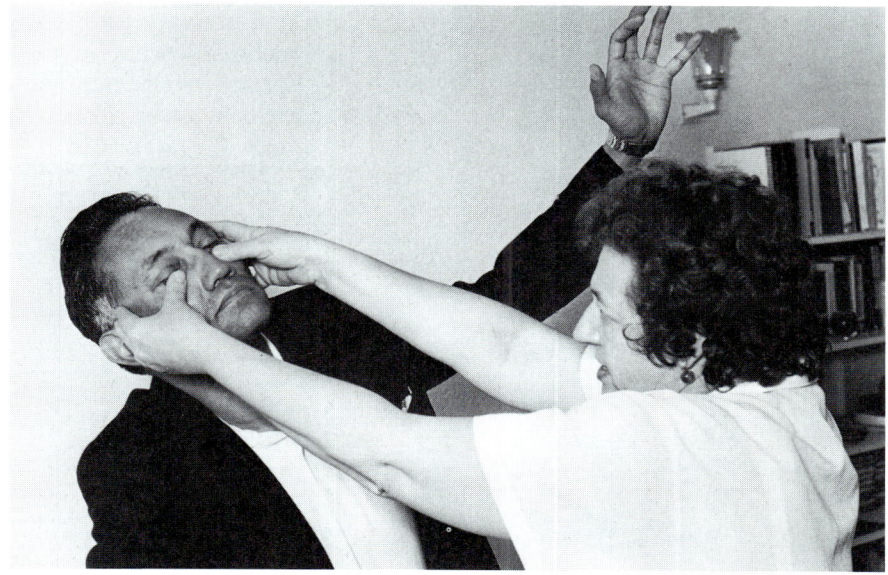

THIEVES

Most thieves will take valuables only if they are easy to get. Don't tempt them by leaving items of value around, just waiting to be stolen.

Only put into your handbag those items you can afford to lose. If you are paid in cash take it straight to the bank or building society; better still arrange to be paid directly into the bank. If you have credit cards, use these instead of cash and keep a separate record of their numbers. If the cards are stolen inform the companies immediately.

Carry your keys in your pocket, then if your bag is stolen, you will still be able to open your front door or car. Remember that the thief will probably be able to find out your address from something in the stolen bag; if your keys are in your pocket then he cannot ransack your home.

If you are going to a very crowded place, such as a market, fun-fair or carnival, consider if you really need to take a bag with you. It may be simpler and safer to leave your money, cheque books and so on at home, and carry a small amount of cash in your pocket along with your keys. If you are sitting in a theatre or cinema, don't push the bag under the seat. Keep it in contact with your body, so that you know its location. The safest place is on your lap.

If you are faced with a thief or number of thieves who threaten physical harm if you do not hand over your bag, then don't fight; just give up the bag.

UMBRELLA DEFENCE

2 Surprised and frightened she instinctively uses her umbrella as a weapon and, swinging her arm well back, she strikes to the side of his head.

1 The thief approaches the girl from behind. As she does not know the man's intentions when he grabs her elbow she assumes that he intends her physical harm. She is walking down a deserted lane and there is no one around to come to her aid. He makes a grab for the bag.

3 He staggers back, dazed. Before he has time to recover his composure, she prepares for the next move.

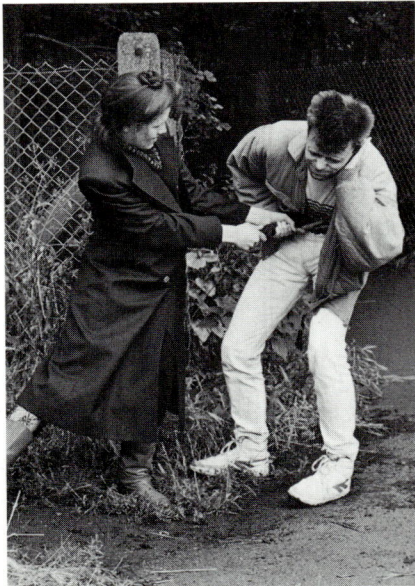

4 Grasping the umbrella firmly in both hands, she jabs him sharply in the stomach with its end.

He is now thoroughly discouraged from making any further attack and she can run safely away.

CHAPTER FOUR

·MARTIAL·ARTS· ·FOR·WOMEN·

IN THE WEST, WE TEND TO SUPPOSE THAT THE ORIENTAL martial arts have been practised by women only during the past decade or so. In fact if we thumb through the pages of Japanese history for more than four centuries, we will be amazed to discover that many ladies of the samurai class were experts in the use of a formidable weapon called the naginata. This ancient, curved-bladed spear was a widely used implement on the battlefields of the early Middle Ages, which, when wielded in arcs, could inflict the most deadly slashes. After it became superseded by the more refined yari, or long straight spear, the wives of the samurai adopted the naginata to defend their homes while their husbands were away at war.

Research into the history of the Chinese martial arts also throws up an interesting fact: the style of kung fu known as Wing Chun is named after the woman who invented it. She herself had been taught the 'plum flower fist' system by a nun from the Shaolin Temple called Ng Mui. Finding this system too complex, with particular emphasis on powerful techniques not altogether suited to the physique of a woman, Yim Wing Chun devised her own style of kung fu purely for self-defence and named it after herself; it means 'beautiful springtime'.

The idea, then, that women are capable human beings well able to look after themselves is not a new one originating with the women's movement. It it true that until the recent past, our western culture tended to emphasize the relative weakness of the female sex, and even today some women may prefer to play the role of a protected species; but this does not have to be everybody's choice. Now we can learn a wide variety of martial skills which will provide us with a supreme sense of well-being and new-found confidence.

BENEFITS OF TRAINING

As you delve into the martial arts, one word that will tend to recur is 'enlightenment'. This immediately suggests a state of mind that is in some way mysteriously religious. Indeed, many martial arts have been closely influenced by Zen Buddhism, but training in the West tends to dismiss the philosophical aspects. Despite this, a change does take place within the student. After two to three years of regular sessions, you will no longer be quite the same woman who first signed on. After repeating particular techniques and adopting various states of mind hundreds of times over to command greater coordination and control, especially in a sparring situation, new patterns of behaviour are gradually absorbed.

EYE CONTACT

You may not suppose that eye movements can play an important part in self-defence, but indeed they can! Western culture has traditionally taught women to play sexual games with their eyes: if their lashes are long and curling, then they can be fluttered alluringly; or else the eyes can be cast down demurely in virginal innocence. Some women are praised by men for having 'bedroom eyes' — often a prelude to seduction. What western society does not do is give approval to women for using their eyes in an assertive manner. In a self-defence context, eye contact plays an enormously important part: a dominant person looks other people directly in the eye, whereas submissive characters tend to look away and can therefore be more easily overpowered. A sudden look away can actually indicate submission. Martial arts pupils therefore learn to look opponents directly in the eye at all times. While doing this, they also learn to use their peripheral vision, so that they know instantly what kind of move to expect next and how to defend themselves against it. Very careful observation of the opponent's eyes can also reveal the exact timing of the next move, because he will tend to narrow them fractionally just before the attack.

If you have always been an introspective sort of person who wanders around either in a vague dream or with your eyes glued to the pavement, then clearly a couple of years of looking threatening opponents calmly in the eye is going to change all that. Your gaze will soon be directed ahead of you, aware at all times what is going on around you, ready to react in any way necessary. As one lady black belt said:

'Using your eyes and ears becomes a habit. Being alert doesn't mean that you're permanently suspicious — that you expect danger around every corner. It simply means that you know what's going on all the time, so you're unlikely to be taken by surprise.'

Sparring is an essential ingredient of most martial arts. In the early stages of learning, this is generally formalized into pre-set sequences of movements, which in karate and taekwon-do consist of an attack followed by a block, which in turn is followed by a counter-attack. Thus the novice can learn to use potentially dangerous techniques in controlled and safe situations, with full cooperation from the sparring partner. Later on, however, it becomes less formalized: the attacker calls out the name of the attack, and the defender can block and counter using any techniques available. Finally the students graduate to free sparring with the aim of scoring points over the opponent. Speed and timing are essential elements in this type of contest. If you consider that an expert in taekwon-do can throw a punch in 3/100 of a second or a kick in 1/10 of a second, then you can imagine how quickly an opponent must react in order to block or evade such a technique. In a real-life self-defence situation, there is no question that a swift, decisive block and counter-attack can save your life. Women's relative lightness of build is a distinct advantage where speed is concerned; their lightning attacks have often outstripped the more cumbersome blocks of their male opponents.

In a sparring situation, concentration is paramount. All the time you are seeking for an opening for a strike, looking for a weakness in your opponent that you can exploit and turn to his disadvantage, while at

SPARRING

Below: *Although shorter in stature and lighter in build, a woman trained in sparring can always find an opening in a male opponent's guard for a swift counter-attack. Here two martial arts experts give a self-defence demonstration.*

the same time ready to block any on-coming attack. This total concentration, a state of calm awareness, in effect replaces fear. While the mind is involved in this detached observation, there is no room for fright. All the energy is directed towards resolving the situation in hand. Women who easily feel afraid or threatened will find this aspect of martial arts training extremely helpful. In competition free sparring, opponents have no idea what punch or kick to expect next, and to this extent the fighting is for real. Rules have been introduced to ensure certain standards of safety, but accidents can occasionally happen simply through misjudged distancing or timing. Adrenalin therefore runs high — an excellent preparation for a real self-defence situation.

In unarmed styles, you also become used to full-power blows being aimed within a millimetre of your nose, solar plexus or other parts of the body and you quickly learn not to flinch. In the weapon art of kendo, actual 'cuts' are made with the bamboo *shinai* or 'sword' on the body, which is protected by armour. Although this sounds fearsome, in fact injuries are extremely rare and there is no doubt that this is a good method for developing courage in combat.

KIME AND KIAI

Above: *A woman's voice can be her best weapon of all. The karate kiai is practised regularly in class until it becomes an automatic part of the student's self-defence equipment.*

At the same time as learning to receive blows, you will also be learning to inflict them. However, it is not enough to perform the techniques using the correct motions and positioning. You also have to demonstrate aggressive fighting spirit and intent of purpose, together with focusing or *kime*. This mental application is extremely important in all the martial arts and makes all the difference to the effectiveness of a technique. Your whole being must be focused into the annihilation of your target.

Most systems also use a penetrating shout, or *kiai*, which is emitted on the point of impact, and which helps to channel all the energy into the attack. It is generated from the lower abdomen through contraction of the muscles which expels the air and sound from the body with considerable force. Such expression of aggression provides a marvellous opportunity for naturally timid women to practise asserting themselves in a truly dynamic way, or for the more extrovert to let off some steam. The kiai in itself is a superb self-defence tool as the following incident demonstrates:

One lady karate brown belt was walking home late one night when she noticed a gang of youths climbing over a bus shelter and generally looking for trouble. She walked past them with all her senses alert and ready for anything. No sooner had she turned her back on them when she heard them whispering something together and the next moment they were all rushing towards her. Immediately she swung round and let out an almighty 'Kiai!' To her enormous surprise the whole lot of them stopped dead in their tracks and then hung about looking rather sheepish.

She was able to walk on in complete confidence, knowing that the psychological tables had been turned. The youths had anticipated the excitement of a chase, but she had let them know in a dramatic way that she wasn't going to play their game. She also discovered that the very act of emitting the kiai helped to dispel her own apprehension.

If you have always wanted a beautiful, sleek figure, then martial arts training is a good way to acquire it. As one lady taekwon-doist said:

> 'Everyone laughed when I started training because I was so fat and unfit. They thought I wouldn't last more than a few weeks. But as the weight began to drop off me, I started to feel fantastic and it was then that I really caught the bug. The buzz that I get from intense training probably isn't any different from the "high" experienced by many athletes, but now I couldn't live without it.'

Whatever she was then, her figure is now well proportioned and trim. A lady karateka agreed:

> 'After three years of training I had dropped from a roomy size 12 to a standard size 10. I particularly lost the weight from my hips and thighs, which I was thrilled about. All the spare flab just vanished. My bosom became firm, too, and my feet, which were positively flat, became well arched. I feel really good about myself now — as if my body is well oiled and will do anything I want it to.'

PHYSICAL PRESENCE

People who study martial arts certainly gain a strong physical presence, whatever their height. A direct gaze, together with an erect but relaxed bearing and streamlined physique all contribute towards this sought-after state. The benefits in everyday life are tremendous, especially for women, who, in a male-dominated society, tend to be at a disadvantage. Lady black belts are truly people to be reckoned with. They are not easily pushed around in business. They know how to stand their ground and deal confidently with difficult situations. Two particularly outstanding characteristics which are immediately noticeable are energy and decisiveness, essential qualities for getting things done.

Together with this good sense of one's own physical body, a feeling of being 'grounded' develops. Oriental people often draw a comparison with a tree; as it draws nourishment from its roots, so a human being can draw power from the earth.

Many types of martial arts such as Shotokan karate place emphasis on low stances, which in addition to strengthening the leg muscles, allow the centre of gravity to drop. This provides stability and good balance, a sound foundation from which to execute difficult techniques. Here women have an inborn advantage: their relatively larger hips give them a lower centre of gravity than men and a naturally good sense of balance, especially valuable for the execution of foot techniques. In a self-defence context, if your knees are bent and your weight dropped downwards, then you will be very hard to push over.

Two common sayings in our own language express similar ideas: a woman who has her two feet 'planted firmly on the ground' is generally regarded as sensible and competent, and one who can 'stand on her own two feet' is independent and able to take care of herself. These are all qualities which can be developed through martial arts training.

BEING GROUNDED

Above: *Denise Rossell-Jones demonstrates the back stance used in the Shotokan style of karate.*

TRAINING Most training sessions begin with some kind of a warm-up and these invariably include exercises with a high aerobic content, such as running and jumping. The spectacular flying kicks of Okinawan karate or Korean taekwon-do can only be achieved with a sound heart and lungs as well as strong, supple muscles. Indeed, considerable importance is attached to correct breathing for all techniques: normally one breathes out towards the moment of impact. This deep, energetic breathing, combined with continued practice of the many arm movements, open up the chest and gives a feeling of expansion. Women who have spent their lives with hunched-up shoulders, crouched over typewriters, or those who have always tended to stoop or hide their feminine curves, will benefit greatly from such exercises. They will find a new sense of personal worth as their chests open up. A well-exercised heart muscle can, of course, cope much better with the general stresses and strains of everyday life.

The fact is that as the body develops and becomes stronger, more supple and better coordinated, a subtle change occurs to the psyche too. Thus the development of body and mind are very closely intertwined. One woman who has dabbled in a number of martial arts and tends to train spasmodically explained how this affected the way she felt about herself:

'I feel tuned up when I'm in training, on top of things, a feeling of being able to cope. I know then that I could do *something* to defend myself. But when I'm out of training, this feeling goes and I'm no longer so sure of myself.'

LINEAR AND CIRCULAR STYLES The movements of the different styles of martial arts can be loosely categorized into two types: linear and circular. Karate, some styles of kung fu, taekwon-do and kendo are all linear in their application, that is they are based on straight punches, kicks, thrusts or cuts, whereas aikido, jiu-jitsu, tai chi and naginata-do employ a circular motion for throws or slashes. The physical training involved in these two categories tends to develop different muscle groups resulting in a somewhat different physique. Although there are more women studying karate than any other form of martial arts, it is said that the circular movements employed in some other systems are particularly well suited to the female body. There is no question that the tough karate and kung fu styles build very strong arm and leg muscles and your biceps and calves will, for instance, become noticeably more developed. The principle behind the circular movements is to use the attacker's own motion and turn it round upon itself. Far less physical strength is therefore needed in an art such as aikido. Generally speaking suppleness and fluidity of motion are important attributes in the circular arts, qualities which women tend to have naturally.

As you progress with your martial arts training, you will find that your stamina will increase enormously. To perfect the techniques and to create quick reactions, all moves are practised hundreds of times over either singly or in short sequences. But perhaps the true test of stamina is the performance of *kata* or patterns. These constitute formalized sets of movements and are generally performed solo. To watch, they are like beautiful, dramatic dances and for many women their performance is the most interesting and satisfying part of the training. The movements represent attacks and blocks against imaginary opponents and the techniques and the way they are linked together become gradually more complicated as the student advances. Nor is it sufficient just to go through the moves; they have to be performed with maximum power, speed and intent and can therefore be really exhausting, but tiredness must never be displayed. Good stamina is a considerable bonus in everyday life, even if you only use it to catch that retreating bus.

A black belt lady instructor in taekwon-do, who has considerable experience of teaching mixed classes, said:

'There is nothing in martial arts training that women can't cope with physically. The only block they have is a mental one, and this usually occurs the first time they are faced with sparring. Men simply love it, because they have been brought up with the rough and tumble of fights ever since they were kids. But women have always been told that they don't get into fights. So they feel enormously inhibited when they are first faced with a fighting situation. They are terrified of hurting someone else and they are terrified of getting hurt themselves. It's a great pity, but I lose a lot of students at this point. Once they get past this, they become very good at the art.' How then did she herself overcome her inhibitions about sparring? 'Oh, sheer pride. I wasn't going to let myself be beaten by this.'

CULTURAL ASPECTS

Women soon realize that they are by no means at a disadvantage when sparring with a man, despite the fact that they have been conditioned to accept the physical superiority of the male. The fact is that women have two particular natural advantages in terms of speed and suppleness. Their innate cunning can also often be brought into play to outwit a male opponent. In forms of unarmed combat, they will quickly discover that a woman's leg can easily outstretch a man's arm, and they soon learn to use foot techniques to their best advantage. Their natural suppleness in the hips more than compensates for lack of height, and even quite short women will have little difficulty in making a foot attack to the head of an average man. They will also be amazed by the power that they can generate with a correctly applied kick. Scientifically, power $=$ speed $\times$ mass, so as long as a woman's techniques are extremely fast, she will produce the necessary power despite her comparative lack of mass. Small people can also get in close, inside the opponent's point of attack. Such realizations can give women a tremendous boost in confidence. They finally come to the conclusion that, despite everything that everyone has ever told them about their physical limitations, they are not in fact inferior to men — just different — and these differences can actually be used to advantage.

Another bonus for women in martial arts training is that they are treated exactly the same as men. They are expected to be just as profi-

Above: *In taekwon-do training, women as well as men are expected to break one-inch (2.5cm) pine boards.*

cient — and therefore they are! A man sparring with a woman will not treat her gently. She is thus forced to put 100 per cent effort into blocking or avoiding attacks and there is no time whatever to consider her femininity. The very act of grappling with men conditions women to become used to their physical presence, their relative height, weight, strength and so on. Such familiarity with the male species gives women a realistic view of what they actually consist of, and this considerably reduces the level of fear in a threatening situation. They also know that every man has a weakness that can be exploited and they can become expert in seeking this out.

Unfortunately a recurring factor which deters women from training is the attitude of boyfriends or husbands. Society has taught them that they are the strong ones, with the muscles to protect their womenfolk. Suddenly they feel their male egos threatened and they forbid their partners to train. Even if such disapproval is not actually voiced, it can be subtly implied and can quickly erode a relationship. If you are faced with this problem, it is best to try and win him round by explaining why you do this and the benefits you are gaining from your study; otherwise his persistent disapproval will gradually weaken your resolve to go training. Lucky are the women with the truly liberated husbands and male friends who are delighted that their partners are looking after their own safety. Even luckier are those who actually train together. Mutual encouragement as well as a spirit of competition will spur both of them on to considerable achievements.

As you gain higher and higher grades in your chosen martial art, you will also notice that other people's attitudes will change towards you. You may have to put up with the ignorant jokes that family and colleagues tend to come up with — such as how many bricks you smash before breakfast — but as you improve, so you will gain in stature, and other people's laughter will gradually be replaced with respect.

CHOOSING A MARTIAL ART

The study of a martial art requires considerable personal commitment. It is not the same as signing on for a keep-fit class, where it matters little if the odd session is missed. Most of the arts demand a very high level of athletic achievement and this is simply not possible if the training is spasmodic. You will have to be prepared to set aside at least two evenings per week for classes and if you really wish to make good progress then home practice is strongly recommended. Some schools insist that you pay for a number of lessons in advance, which of course encourages regular attendance.

If you take up tai chi chuan, then you will have to pay for a whole term in advance and attend every week without fail. This is because you are required to learn the tai chi form, which is a long solo pattern of movements that takes many weeks to absorb. Each week a new part of the form will be added to the sequences already taught and the students progress at the same rate. Clearly, if you miss a class you will also miss an important part of the sequence and you will fall behind. Although you will probably attend the school only once a week, you will need to practise the form every day at home — even if only for ten minutes — otherwise you will find it impossible to remember.

All this may sound like an awful effort, but the fact is that once you become totally absorbed by your chosen art — and you soon will — nothing will keep you away from the training hall. Not only is it totally fascinating, described by one instructress as 'like a box without a bottom — always something new to be discovered', but it is also tremendous fun. There is something enormously liberating about launching yourself from the floor into a flying side-kick or beating the hell out of a punch bag, or in expressing yourself through those large, expansive movements. Many women find the study of kata or patterns particularly pleasing, since aesthetics come into play here too in the form of rhythm and perfection of style; the rewards are therefore very similar to those of dancing. Most clubs have a friendly atmosphere and you will often find the more senior male students particularly encouraging and helpful.

The best advice is to be circumspect about your choice of martial art. Take your time. Study the advertisements in your local newspaper or in the martial arts magazines. Find out all you can about the arts which appeal to you most, then arrange to go and watch classes. It is also important to ensure that teachers are bona fide before signing on, and that they are registered with the controlling body in your country (such as The Martial Arts Commission in Great Britain). If so, then your gradings will be recognized internationally and you will be covered by insurance in the event of an injury.

Injuries in fact are surprisingly rare, but to a certain extent their frequency is determined by the type of art you choose. For instance, if you decide on tai chi, then the chances of injuring yourself are probably as low as in the study of yoga. If on the other hand you are attracted by the ferocity of Thai boxing, then you will have to expect the odd broken nose. Full contact karate, otherwise known as kick-boxing, is a sport developed in the West and not a true Oriental martial art. Padded armour is worn and full-power blows are inflicted on the opponent's body in order to win points. Unless you have a particularly blood-

Above: *Women karateka compete internationally and the kata event is always hotly contested. In this photograph, a member of the US team demonstrates her expertise at the World Karate Championships in Holland.*

thirsty bent, then this is frankly a distinctly risky route to effective self-defence for women. Nearly all of the true unarmed arts teach the pulling of kicks and punches to within a fraction of the target, so that actual contact is not made. The effectiveness of a strike can always be tested on a punch bag, or on a *makiwara* (a padded punching post), or in taekwon-do and karate, in the breaking of boards. If you are worried about an accidental blow on the breast, you can protect yourself with a specially reinforced bra available by mail order, as advertised in the martial arts magazines.

The following descriptions cover the most popular martial arts, and they will give you a good idea what to expect from the training. Some are more rigorous than others and some are better suited to women's bodies. Effective self-defence will be acquired either very quickly or only after years of training. Obviously, the choice depends on your own needs and tastes together with the availability of classes in your own locality. You may also feel more confident if other women are attending in good numbers. You may prefer to try out different styles before making a final decision. But whichever art you eventually decide on, if you study it for any reasonable length of time, then you can be sure it will change your life.

AIKIDO

The word aikido means 'the way of all harmony'. By harmonizing with the energy of the attacker, it is possible to re-direct and overcome it. This process has been described in terms of throwing a brick at a curtain; the curtain yields at the impact, but in doing this it also absorbs the force of the flying brick, which can then only drop to the floor, all energy spent.

The art was founded comparatively recently by the Japanese Morihei Ueshiba and many of the locks, holds, and strikes to weak points are derived from jiu-jitsu. It is a highly effective form of self-defence and many of the techniques are used by police forces around the world. It is an art particularly suited to women, because it relies on the skilful twisting of joints to bring about a submission rather than the brute force of, say, karate.

There are various schools of aikido but women will probably find that the traditional style, with its softer approach relying on full co-operation from the partner, will suit them best. It can certainly be most beautiful to watch with its graceful, fluid movements and the swirling of the long divided skirts worn by the higher grades. However, it should be pointed out that it takes longer to acquire effective self-defence techniques from this method than from the Tomiki or Yoshinkan schools. The Tomiki style incorporates competitive and sporting aspects; in one-to-one combat an attacker will use a rubber knife to attempt to stab a victim, who then has to evade and turn the knife to his own advantage, perhaps by twisting the attacker's wrist and turning the weapon against his throat. The Yoshinkan school in particular teaches *atemi* strikes, or strikes to the vulnerable parts of the body. These are of especial use to women, because very little strength is required to inflict a deadly blow to one of these vital points. The concept of correct distancing is also practised, together with evasive movement, so the defender is close by but safe from the attacker.

Above: *The lady on the right performs a wrist throw (kote-gaeshi) on her opponent. The lock uses his own weight and momentum.*

You will find an air of quiet discipline in the aikido *dojo* or training hall. The class will begin with warming-up exercises which will place emphasis on loosening the joints. The wrists in particular must be supple because they will be grabbed and twisted quite a lot during training. Roll-outs will also be practised, whereby the student literally dives on to the mats and rolls over the forward arm on to the back, the spine curved and head tucked in, then up on to the feet. These are essential because throws form an important part of aikido technique. Students then pair up to practise basic locks, holds and the throws. If too much pressure is being put on a trapped joint, then the student can indicate submission by a slap on the thigh, at which the hold is released.

Kata, or prearranged movements between two partners, are also practised to produce perfect mastery of technique.

Every few months gradings will be carried out in which students are tested in proficiency and coloured belts are awarded in some styles, until finally the first degree (*dan*) of black belt is reached denoting junior instructor grade. Until this point, white cotton suits are worn.

A considerable number of women study aikido and many of these reach high grades.

ELBOW LOCK

1 By extending her arms away from her body, the woman releases herself from the bear hug.

2 She steps to the side, creating an opening, meanwhile pushing away the attacker's left hand by extending her arm. At the same time she grasps his other wrist above her shoulder.

3 By stepping under and back, she twists his arm and attacks his elbow joint cutting it in a forward arc. She then forces him on to the floor, controlling his body all the time through his elbow.

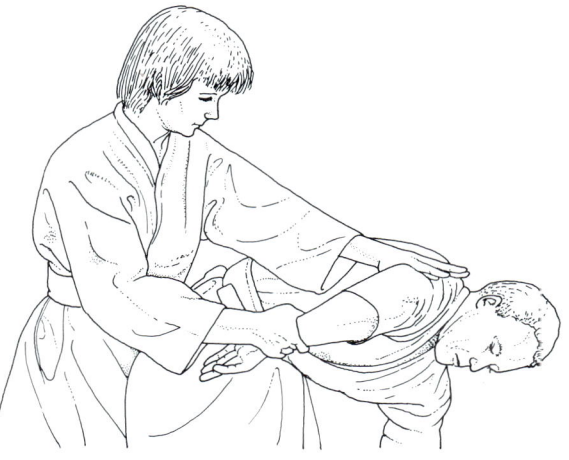

HAPKIDO

This art is Korean in origin, but its principles are very similar to aikido — in fact the word also means 'way of all harmony'. Unfortunately, classes are not well distributed; there is a far better choice of schools in America than in Britain, but its self-defence potential is so good that it would be well worth trying to seek one out. In addition to the yielding and deflection principles, there is a syllabus of powerful attacks incorporating the spectacular Korean jumping kicks. Modern exponents give demonstrations, especially of breaking techniques, but the emphasis in training is always on self-defence rather than the sporting aspects.

Just as in aikido, an attack is met without direct resistance. Skilled deflection techniques guide the attacking limb beyond the target and then the defender's own motion is added to it, which causes the attacker to lose his balance and it is then easy to take him into a throw. Alternatively if the attacker grasps his victim, a pressure-point strike is used to weaken the hold, and it is then broken by twisting against the joints. The repertoire of techniques is vast, but a student can select those that are most useful or best-suited to her particular physique.

Gradings are held every three months and students advance through the *kups* before reaching dan status. The practice suit is either dark in colour, or else dark trousers are worn with a light top.

Right: *Circular kicks form part of the repertoire of the hapkidoist.*

JIU-JITSU

This is an ancient art with origins in strife-ridden medieval Japan, when techniques were devised which exploited the joints in the opponents' armour by twisting and grasping the limbs until they were rendered helpless.

The art is mainly concerned with effective and practical self-defence systems, many of which are of particular interest to women requiring as they do little strength, but producing devastating results. For those who are extremely squeamish about hurting people or worried about actually killing them, then restraining techniques can be selected which prevent an attacker from using violence without causing him any real damage. For this reason, jiu-jitsu techniques are widely employed by prison officers and policemen and -women around the world. You still have to be sure, however, that you can get away safely afterwards.

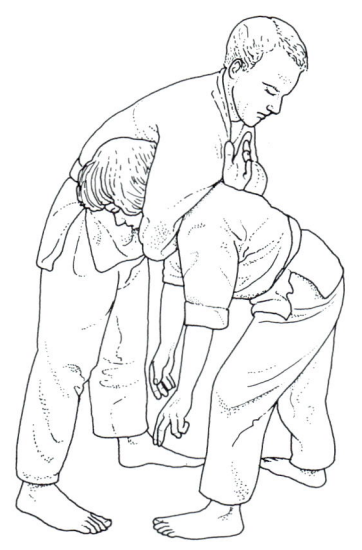 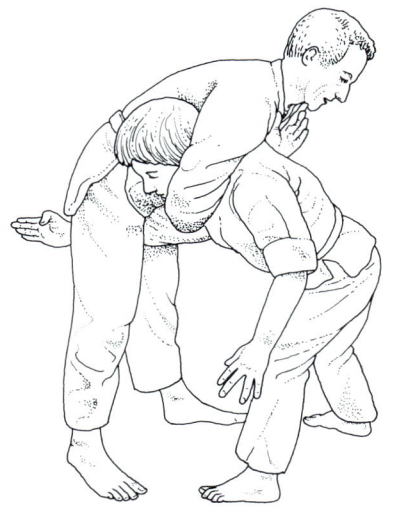 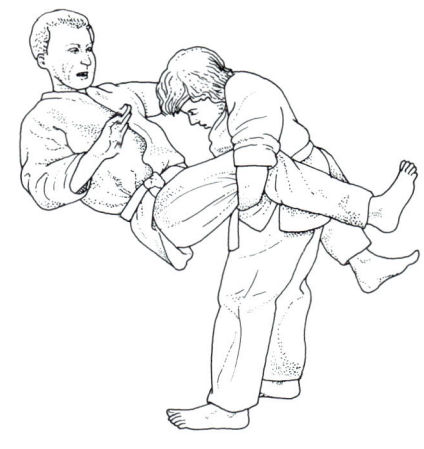

ESCAPE FROM SIDE HEAD-LOCK

1 The man holds his victim securely in a side head-lock.

2 The woman causes her attacker to slacken his grip by striking upwards with her forearm into his groin. Notice the tensed fingers.

3 She grabs him behind the knees and by pulling sharply upwards and backwards, he falls to the ground. In training, jiu-jitsu students learn how to fall safely.

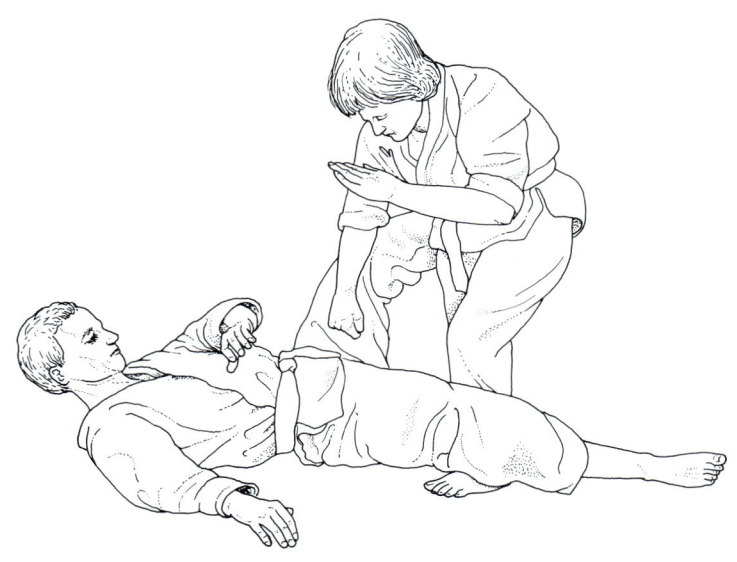

4 She finishes off her attacker by punching into his groin. Many jiu-jitsu techniques are very dangerous, such as this one.

The basic principle of this art is the same as in aikido (which was derived from it), and that is compliance; indeed, the name means 'compliant techniques'. Rather than contesting the force used against you (in which case the stronger person will win), you comply with it, so that if an attacker pushes, you pull, and if he pulls, you push. There are also techniques for initiating an attack if necessary, and these include distraction strikes to vital points. These are followed up by throws or locks. There are also a few low-target kicks. Even the simplest of holds and locks, especially those applied to the fingers, can cause the most excruciating pain and all can be carried out by people of small build.

The main advantage of jiu-jitsu is that the entire syllabus is so wide, that every possible type of attack and defence is covered and there is an enormous range of techniques to choose from. The disadvantage is that it takes a long time to assimilate.

Although you will find the training rigorous, the athletic skills required for the high kicks needed in other martial arts do not apply here. All jiu-jitsu techniques can be used wearing ordinary clothes, although it should be pointed out that very tight skirts or high heels that restrict the movements or upset the balance can be a disadvantage.

Jiu-jitsu stresses the use of available objects as weapons, which can be picked up spontaneously in dangerous situations. For instance, a dustbin lid can be of assistance in defence against a knife attack, or a handful of gravel can be thrown into the attacker's face.

Women find the groundwork section especially useful, because this teaches escape from prone positions — not included in many of the other martial arts.

There are plenty of jiu-jitsu schools in the West and women are made welcome.

JUDO

Although judo is considered to be a sport rather than a martial art, it is included here partly because of its popularity and partly because many of the techniques can be used in self-defence situations. In essence, it is a sporting version of jiu-jitsu with all the really dangerous techniques, especially the atemi strikes, excluded.

Judo, 'the compliant way', was founded by a jiu-jitsu expert named Jigoro Kano. He had been a weak child, persistently suffering from ill health, who had taken up martial arts to help him become stronger. At that time, jiu-jitsu was earning itself something of a bad name. Schools had opened up which were teaching commoners, as opposed to the warrior class, and some of these students were misusing the techniques learnt to terrorize the public on the streets. Kano, who had studied the classical jiu-jitsu as taught to the warrior caste, did not want to be associated with such bullies, and he changed the name of his own style to Kodokan Judo. His art encouraged sporting competition in which the two opponents had to show respect for each other.

Timing, alertness, distancing and so forth are all important in judo as in any type of self-defence, and these are all well worth acquiring. *Randori*, which consists of a free exchange of techniques between sparring partners, is an important element of the practice and this develops lightning responses. However, since judo is mainly a sport, women tend to work together with someone of their own weight and size and have less opportunity for pitting their skills against men of any weight or size. This of course restricts the self-defence potential.

Throws, locks and holds are all part of the course, all of which can be of use in a street situation. However, the sport is criticized for being sometimes impractical. For instance, throws need a large amount of space and they won't help you if you are attacked in a telephone booth. Also, your opponent has to grasp you in a particular way in order for your response to be effective.

Judo is widely practised by women, who compete at international level, and there are many clubs all over the western world. A heavy white cotton suit is worn for practice and students progress through coloured belts up to the degrees of black belt.

If it is the sport which mainly interests you, then by all means go for judo, but if you really want to learn to defend yourself effectively, then jiu-jitsu will be a far better choice.

The popular idea about karate is that its practitioners spend most of their time smashing bricks and boards. In fact breaking techniques are not part of the general syllabus at all below black belt. So don't let this image put you off. In fact karate consists of a highly efficient system of unarmed combat (the word karate means 'empty hand' or karate-do means 'way of the empty hand') and many techniques can be used very effectively for self-defence. Indeed it was devised by Okinawans to protect themselves against marauders, after the carrying of weapons had been banned by their Japanese rulers. Gichin Funakoshi was the man who brought Okinawa-te to Japan in 1923 and the karate that we know today began to develop.

The techniques consist mainly of high-energy strikes and kicks and students practise these first of all in lines before pairing up with a sparring partner. Although the scope of the system is nothing like as comprehensive as jiu-jitsu, for instance there are very few throws and virtually no groundwork, it is possible to learn effective kicks, punches and blocks fairly quickly, which can be of considerable use in a self-defence situation.

Karate is probably the most popular of the martial arts and is practised worldwide, with a considerable number of female participants. This is despite the fact that it is reckoned to be a 'hard' martial art, one that relies on muscle power for its effect and one that is offensive rather than defensive. There is no doubt that the kicks are of great value to women. You learn to deliver them in all directions and at all levels, front, back and to the side, down to the foot as well as up to the head. A fast snapping action is acquired, so that the opponent is unable to catch the kicking foot, and the move is initiated from the hip with the weight of the whole body thrust into the attack. In a front kick, the striking area is the ball of the foot, so the toes have to be pulled back. The side kick uses the edge of the foot as a powerful thrusting instrument. For close-up confrontations, the knee becomes the weapon. Women also find the elbow strikes very useful in self-defence situations.

Above: *This body drop* (taiotoshi) *is a classic judo throw using leverage rather than strength.*

KARATE

KNIFE-HAND BLOCK AND COUNTER-ATTACK

1 The woman defends herself against a front kick with a downward knife-hand block. At the same time she steps away from her attacker.

2 She changes her weight on to the other foot and performs a karate chop to the back of his neck.

COUNTER-ATTACK WITH ELBOW

1 The girl evades a front punch by stepping to the side and blocking with her wrist. At the same time she jabs her attacker in the ribs with her left hand.

2 She then steps in towards the man and counter-attacks with her elbow (*empi*) under his chin.

The novice may well be confused by the number of different styles practised. The most popular is Shotokan which uses low stances and very powerful techniques. Perhaps better suited to a woman's build is Wado-ryu, which is lighter and faster with somewhat higher stances. Evasion is often favoured over direct blocking techniques, which can leave the forearms and shins covered in bruises. Shotokai is also a softer style in that there is no competition fighting, but it uses low stances similar to Shotokan. Kyokushinkai is very hard and strenuous with emphasis on breaking techniques. It incorporates a particularly ruthless form of competition called 'knockdown' in which full-contact blows and kicks to the body and head are allowed in order to knock the competitor to the ground. It is not necessary to go to such lengths to learn effective self-defence and this style is not recommended here for women. Goju-ryu is also more suitable for men with its use of weights to condition the body. For instance, huge earthenware pots full of stones have to be lifted and carried. Shukokai has been developed more recently with a particular emphasis on power. Techniques are tested against absorbent pads held by the partner — a useful way of gauging the impact of a blow.

Women certainly excel in the performance of kata which are rather like powerful, dramatic dances, incorporating a wide variety of techniques. Competitions are held at international level and these can be most inspiring to watch. After agitation from a number of groups, women are now also allowed to compete in free-fighting contests.

Every three months or so students enter for gradings which are conducted mainly in Japanese. Techniques have to be demonstrated, together with pre-arranged sparring and the performance of kata. More advanced students have to show their skills in semi-free or contest free-fighting. Beginners fasten their suits with white belts, after which they progress to yellow, then green, purple, brown and black. It is therefore possible to dye the same belt a darker colour with each new grade! All standards train together, the class sometimes forming groups with beginners at one end and the more advanced at the other. Beginners can benefit greatly from watching the senior students train.

Respect is shown at all times to the teacher and the more senior students. It is customary to bow on entering and leaving the *dojo*, eyes always looking ahead, and all training sessions begin and end with a kneeling bow. Before this last bow, it is usual to spend a few minutes meditating to clear and calm the mind.

KENDO

Although the techniques of kendo are highly specialized, and not really relevant to a modern self-defence situation, the mental qualities developed by the training are well worth acquiring, and for this reason the art has been included in this list.

The word means 'way of the sword', but real swords have long been substituted by the *shinai*, a light-weight bamboo weapon with a handguard and grip at one end, developed purely for safe practice. A helmet and body armour are worn, so that full-power cuts can be made against the opponent.

Kendo was actively encouraged by the Japanese government between the World Wars and a controlling body was set up to establish rules for competition and kata to be practised. Today kendo is popular throughout the world with a considerable number of female participants.

Fighting spirit is developed right from the start by pairing up the novice with a higher grade. The new student has to attack the senior grade repeatedly. Apart from aggression, this also gives practice in technique and correct distancing. When scoring a point, the student must shout out its name: *'men'* to the head, *'do'* to the breastplate, *'kote'* to the gauntlets or *'tsuki'*, a thrust to the throat.

It is essential to be able to distinguish a real attack from a feint, so that it can be diverted and, with practice, kendoka become extremely quick and alert. A good kendo competition can be positively ferocious to watch, while the black armour and long *hakama* (divided skirt) provide a dramatic touch.

Above: *The lady kendoka on the left is about to make a cut to the do (breastplate) of her opponent.*

KUNG FU

After Bruce Lee shot to stardom in the 1970s with *Enter the Dragon*, young people were enrolling in their droves at their local *kwoons* (training halls) and training in Chinese martial arts was at last becoming freely available in the West. Nevertheless, some authentic masters still teach Chinese students only and much is kept secret. It is hard to assess, therefore, how many styles of Chinese martial arts actually exist.

Their precise origins are lost in the mists of time, but it seems that the monks of the Shaolin Temple in the Hunan province of China had a profound influence on their development in the form of Chinese boxing, which they practised as much for good health as for self-defence.

Your choice of kung fu style will almost certainly be governed by whatever happens to be available in your area. Generally speaking, styles from northern China, such as Shaolin Fists, are regarded as 'hard', with long stances and emphasis on kicks. Hands are conditioned on a wooden dummy. Many women may find these styles too severe. Southern styles, like Wing Chun, are less athletic and more practical in their application.

Wing Chun techniques are direct and economical and there are only three set forms to learn. A good basis for self-defence can therefore be acquired very quickly. The principle is to cover your centre-line at all times (an imaginary line running down the centre of the body) and thus the vital points are always protected. Kicks are usually low, making use of the heel as a powerful weapon, as well as the side of the foot. If you watch a performance of one of the forms, you will be particularly impressed with the speed of the hand movements which combine deflecting with grabbing and pulling. Thus a block can be instantly followed up by a counter-attack. This style of kung fu is ideal for close confrontations where there may be little room for movement.

SPARRING

1 The man blocks the woman's straight punch with his wrist. Notice that her left hand keeps guard while the right goes into the attack.

2 He immediately follows up with a front kick, but the woman deflects this by twisting her arm over and sweeping it away to her right. She continues to guard her face.

3 The man throws a punch, but as he moves in, the woman blocks with her right hand while striking to his eyes with her fingertips.

Praying Mantis has both northern and southern schools, but both emphasize grabbing and pulling, thus exposing vital points to strike. The grab is effected with the hand shaped like a mantis' claw.

Several styles use techniques based on animal or bird movements, such as the Crane and Tiger system or Hung Gar. This is a low, powerful style requiring stamina and strong legs. Some girls do take it up, but not all classes are open to westerners. The Mischievous Monkey system, as its name implies, uses ape-like movements with emphasis on speed and agility.

Another interesting system is Choy Lee Fut which demonstrates wide movements and long stretches of the arms. Women have found many of the techniques useful for self-defence, although traditional Chinese weapons are incorporated into the training.

If you come across the term *wu shu*, this simply refers to Chinese war arts in general, particularly as studied in the modern People's Republic. Training tends to be highly gymnastic, requiring both agility and grace.

Traditional kung fu masters teach on an individual basis through their senior students and there are no grades as such. A westernized *sifu* (master) may, however, teach the students in rank and offer the encouragement of coloured belts. Often there is no special uniform, a T-shirt and loose Chinese trousers being the most usual dress.

NAGINATA-DO

Unfortunately, classes are hard to find in the West at present, although naginata-do has long been tremendously popular among women in Japan, especially in the colleges. Your nearest kendo club will be the best source of information for details about training in your area.

Like kendo, the study of the naginata develops good timing, alertness, fighting spirit and many other qualities that are of vital importance in self-defence. When pitted against male kendoka, the ladies wielding the naginatas are nearly always the winners; they make up for their relative lack of strength by using speed and flexibility. Kata is an important element and circular movements predominate. These are said to be very beneficial for a woman's body, providing even muscle tone.

Like the shinai of kendo, the live blade of the naginata has been replaced with bamboo, plaited into a curve to resemble the original shape. The uniform is also similar to that worn by the kendoka, with a thick cotton jacket and hakama.

As the most ancient form of women's self-defence, naginata-do is of especial interest — a martial art that has evolved mainly for ladies.

Above: *Two students of naginata-do practise sparring.*

SHORINJI KEMPO

This is a modern Japanese martial art founded by Doshin So in the post-war years to help rebuild the morale of the nation's youth. He himself had learnt Shaolin kung fu while living in China and the basis of the system is derived from this, with many new additions.

There are about 700 techniques, both hard and soft, which cover every possible situation for defending oneself, and since skill and scientific application are considered more important than size or physical strength the system is suitable for women and for older people.

The emphasis is always on defence, with any counter-attack used only as a last resort. The study of pressure applied to 142 vital ponts is basic to this system, as is cooperative training with a partner to identify pain thresholds. At the end of each session *seiho*, a form of massage, is practised, which relieves stress to the muscles and joints and leaves the students feeling relaxed and fresh.

Although the more extreme religious aspects are not adhered to in the West, moral principles are considered important, such as the ideal that students should strive to be balanced human beings in harmony with others. Unfortunately, classes are not always well distributed.

TAEKWON-DO

There are basically two types of taekwon-do: that controlled by the ITF (International Taekwon-do Federation) and then there is the WTF (World Taekwon-do Federation). This latter style allows full-contact kicks and punches, and body armour is worn for protection, but despite this injuries are common. In ITF competition SAF'T' pads over the insteps and knuckles are obligatory, but these are to protect one's partner from accidental blows, since all punches and kicks are pulled. The ITF style is in fact a highly suitable form of self-defence for women and female participation is encouraged. Many women now hold black belts and compete in the international arena.

Training is, however, vigorous and a commitment to a minimum of twice-weekly sessions is essential. Warm-ups last about 30 minutes, starting with general loosening such as twisting from the waist, knee bends and so on, then exercises with a high aerobic content follow, for example running for about two minutes, star jumps for the same length of time, then leap-frogs over a line of people. Specific muscle groups are

Right: *The flying kicks of taekwon-do are truly spectacular, but take years of training to perfect.*

RELEASE FROM A GRAB

3 A punch to the ribs finally causes the man to loosen his grip.

This sequence is typical of some of the practical self-defence techniques incorporated into the taekwon-do syllabus.

1 The man has grabbed the woman by the wrist, but she does not pull away.

2 Instead she steps in and executes an upper strike with the elbow to his chin.

worked on to develop strength — arms, legs and stomach — with perhaps 20 V-sits. Stretching follows warm-ups, and this is always closely supervised.

Many techniques are similar to karate, especially the hand strikes, and basic training is in rank. A considerable number of the kicks, such as the reverse turning kick, the twisting kick, split kick and twin foot kicks are, however, truly Korean in origin and are quite spectacular to observe. Emphasis is also placed on the patterns which become increasingly difficult as the students progress through the coloured belts up to degrees of black belt.

Ladies are treated exactly the same as men, except that they are not expected to build up callouses on their hands and feet. They are, however, expected to perform destruction techniques and these are regarded as an important part of the training. No one can be aware of the true effectiveness of their strikes until they are tested against a piece of pine. At first ladies are taught to break with their feet and shoes are allowed for training purposes. In fact speed rather than strength is the essential ingredient and women are always amazed by the power they can generate.

The founder of taekwon-do, General Choi, has spent his whole life analysing and refining this modern Korean martial art. The result is a 15-volume encyclopedia which catalogues 3,200 techniques. His scientific approach has produced a highly efficient form of self-defence, combined with movements which are aesthetically pleasing. The study of vital points is included in the training syllabus as is the choice of the correct weapon for each different target. A striving towards positive moral rearmament is also considered important and five tenets must be upheld: courtesy, integrity, perseverance, self-control and indomitable spirit.

The uniform is similar to a karate suit but is distinguished by a black braid trim. Strict discipline is expected in the *do jang* (training hall) and instructors must be treated with respect and referred to as Sir or Ma'am.

There is no doubt that a competent taekwon-doist will not be afraid to walk around on her own at night.

TAI CHI CHUAN

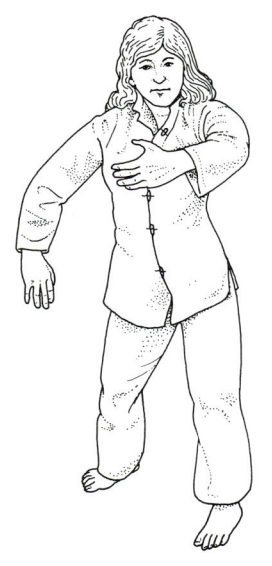

Above: *A move from the Short Form of tai chi chuan.*

This is an ancient Chinese exercise based on Taoist philosophy, which probably originated some 4,000 years ago, with a name that means 'grand ultimate boxing'. Through the meditative dance-like form, you lose your ego and become one with nature (or Tao). Thus the soft, weak and yielding overcomes the hard, strong and unyielding. In other words, by yielding before an attacker's force, a mere pull or push, correctly applied, can cause him to fall to the ground. Immediate benefits are increased relaxation, the attainment and maintenance of good mental, spiritual and physical health, a longer life and a happier existence. The self-defence aspect is very much a secondary benefit because it takes so many years to reach a real level of proficiency, but for those with the dedication, its potential is without equal.

Women have a natural advantage because they have an inborn sensitivity and softness which men generally do not possess. They must, however, gradually increase their strength and skill. This is achieved first of all through the practice of the solo form. It may take a whole year to perfect the shortened version of the form, which consists of many different movements with poetic names such as 'White Crane Spreading Wings' or 'Embrace Tiger and Return to Mountain'. Although many of these contain punches, kicks and deflecting techniques, they are always very softly performed in a fluid and relaxed manner. You will probably be expected to commit yourself to one class each week, with a 10-minute practice session at home every day.

It is well worth persevering to the next stage, the Pushing-Hands practice, which is performed with a partner. The object is to uproot your opponent so that both his feet leave the ground, while remaining rooted yourself. Being rooted is an important concept in tai chi, which is achieved through complete relaxation, a low centre of gravity and the mental image of the weight permeating the earth. Light contact is maintained all the time with your opponent, and, using moves from the form, you yield to the slightest pressure, or stick to him when he retreats. Persistent practice will provide an appreciation of the difference between the forceful energy of the muscles and the intrinsic, tenacious energy released by the mind. These can be compared to the difference between a rigid stick or a pliable vine. Eventually, you will be able to anticipate your opponent's moves before he makes them.

The *chi* in the name is the Chinese equivalent of *ki*, the potential energy discussed in more down-to-earth terms in the chapter How to Fight Back, which gives simple exercises to demonstrate its use. You may sometimes hear tai chi referred to as an 'internal' style of kung fu, through which the inner energy is developed, as opposed to the 'external' styles which depend on the force of the muscles. Tai chi is a particularly good choice for elderly or weak people, since no age limit is imposed.

More of a sport than a martial art as such, Thai boxing is fiercely aggressive and competitive, with no set patterns to learn, no philosophy for the improvement of the character, and the emphasis always on pure fighting. Injuries are common and ladies as well as men have to be prepared to take blows to the body. There is no doubt about the effectiveness of the techniques for self-defence purposes, but the training is extremely gruelling and not for the faint-hearted.

Muay Thai, as it is called in its homeland, has been popular for centuries, ever since a king declared that all people should learn the unarmed combat arts practised by the military. Village boxing events took place on a regular basis, until finally in 1931 it became a national sport and rules were introduced to eliminate the more deadly blows and reduce the risk of injury.

Although originally based on Chinese boxing, many techniques are peculiar to Thailand, particularly the close-range tactics involving the use of the elbow, knee and shin. Footwork and leg movements are very important, presenting a constantly moving target to the opponent — more difficult to attack than a static one. Stamina is therefore gradually built up, with running and swimming frequently included in the training regimen.

Boxing matches take place in a ring and they always begin with a ritualistic dance. Gloves are worn, but there is no other protective clothing — just a T-shirt and shorts, allowing freedom of movement.

Despite the bloodthirsty nature of the sport, women now compete internationally, although they were traditionally banned from the ring as they were thought to bring bad luck. Western clubs at present are mostly based in the north of England and some parts of Holland, Germany and France.

THAI BOXING

Above: *The boxer on the left performs a flying knee attack.*

DO MARTIAL SKILLS WORK?

Debbie Wynne-Kwoo, a taekwon-do instructress for the ITF, holding a black belt, was walking along the pavement one evening in a small English town. Without provocation, two guys came up behind her and grabbed her. She had no idea who they were and she didn't wait to find out, but swung round and let loose a front fist punch to the solar plexus of the larger of the two. 'It was amazing', she exclaimed. 'It felt like hitting a bag of feathers. He just crumpled up and dropped to the ground. His mate ran off and I leapt into a passing taxi.' The taxi driver, having witnessed this astonishing scene, told the local papers and Debbie hit the headlines. The membership of her club rose rapidly.

Most lady martial artists, however, never have to test their physical skills in this way. As they will all tell you, they are so alert and tuned up with the constant training, that would-be muggers and rapists simply never get near enough to do any damage. Should they be taken by surprise, they have sufficient confidence in their techniques to know that they can defend themselves.

The most important point, however, is that they no longer feel terrorized by men and can walk the streets without fear. This gives them a marvellous sense of liberation, knowing they have the freedom to live their lives in whatever way they choose.

USEFUL INFORMATION AND ADDRESSES

GREAT BRITAIN

Austin Goh Martial Arts Centre,
7 Langley Street, London WC2.
Tel: 01-240 6777
(Training in Wing Chun kung fu
and tai chi.)

All Europe Taekwon-do Federation,
36 Woodberry Avenue, North
Harrow, Middlesex HA2 6AX.
Tel: 01-863 0664

British Aikido Board,
Mrs S. Timms, 6 Halkingcroft,
Langley, Slough, Berkshire.

British Kung Fu Council,
Oakdale Avenue, Pinner Road,
Northwood, Middlesex HA6 1PG.

British Pregnancy Advisory Service,
Austy Manor, Wootton Wawen,
Solihull, West Midlands B95 6BX.
Tel: 05642 3225

British Self-Defence Association,
4th Floor, 20-22 Shelton Street,
London WC2.

Brook Advisory Centres,
153a East Street, London SE17 2SD.
Tel: 01-708 1234

Child Assault Prevention
Programme, 30 Windsor Court,
Moscow Road, London W2 4SN.
(Classes for schools organized
on request.)

Criminal Injuries Compensation
Board, 19-30 Alfred Place,
London WC1E 7LG.
Tel: 01-636 9501

D.A.W.N. (Drugs Alcohol and
Women Nationally), Boundary
House, 91-93 Charterhouse Street,
London EC1M 6HR.

English Karate Council, 1st Floor,
Broadway House, 15/16 Deptford
Broadway, London SE8 4PE.

Family Planning Association,
26-35 Mortimer Street,
London W1N 7RJ.
Tel: 01-636 7866

Incest Crisis Line
There is a network of crisis lines
around Britain. Check telephone
directory, or ring enquiries for
your local number.
The London numbers are
01-422 5100 and 01-890 4732.

International Tai Chi Chuan
Association, 184/192 Drummond
Street, London NW1.
Tel: 01-387 5381

The Martial Arts Commission,
Broadway House, 15-16 Deptford
Broadway, London SE8 4PA.
Tel: 01-691 3433
(Gives information on martial arts
clubs and self-defence training.)

The Metropolitan Special
Constabulary, New Scotland Yard,
London SW1H 0BG.
(Provides free self-defence training
to groups of women in London.)

National College of Karate and
Martial Arts, 80 Judd Street,
London WC1.
Tel: 01-837 4406
(Karate and hapkido; self-defence.)

National Marriage Guidance
Council, Herbert Gray College,
Little Church Street,
Rugby CV21 3AP.
Tel: 0788-73 241

Pregnancy Advisory Service,
11-13 Charlotte Street,
London W1P 1HD.
Tel: 01-637 8962

Rape Crisis Centres
There are many centres in the
larger towns. Check telephone
directory, or ring enquiries,
for your local number.

Samaritans
Check telephone directory, or ring
enquiries, for your local number.

Shotokan Karate Centre,
Marshall Street Baths,
Marshall Street, London W1.
Tel: 01-734 0900

Women Against Rape, King's Cross
Women's Centre, 71 Tonbridge
Street, London WC1H 9DZ.
Tel: 01-837 7509; mail to
P.O. Box 287, London NW6 5QU.
WAR is a member of the
International Wages for
Housework Campaign, which also
includes:
　English Collective of Prostitutes
　International Black Women for
　　Wages for Housework
　Legal Action for Women
　Wages Due Lesbians
　WinVisible: Women with Visible
　　and Invisible Disabilities
All these organizations can be
contacted at the King's Cross
Women's Centre (see above).

Women's Aid Federation,
373 Gray's Inn Road, London WC1.
Tel: 01-837 9316

Women's Self-Defence (UK) Ltd,
Freepost BS3301, Bristol BS14 0BR.
Tel: 0272 836467

Women's Therapy Centre,
6 Manor Gardens, London N7 6LA.
Tel: 01-263 6200

World Jiu Jitsu Federation,
Barlow Lane, Fazakerley,
Liverpool 9.
Tel: 051-523 9611

WEA (Workers' Educational
Association), National Office,
Temple House, 9 Upper Berkeley
Street, London W1H 8BT.
(Phone or write for local branch
details. They often run courses in
assertiveness training.)

Further education centres and extra-mural departments of universities also run self-defence and assertiveness courses, so check with your local education department or library.

AUSTRALIA

There are women's services, pregnancy and related services in the larger cities, listed in telephone directories.

Marriage counselling services are widely available.

There are also large numbers of self-defence and martial arts clubs. Information can be obtained from The Federation of Australian Karate-Do Organizations, Trades Hall Building, 4 Gouldborne Street, Sydney 2000, N.S.W.

CANADA

Canadian Association of Sexual Assault Centres, 77 East 20th Avenue, Vancouver B.C. V5V 1L7. Tel: 604-872 8212

Rape crisis centres, refuges from violence, family services, and women's services are listed in telephone directories for the larger cities.

There are also large numbers of self-defence and martial arts clubs. Information can be obtained from The National Karate Association, Box 788, Station F, Toronto, Ontario, N4Y 2N7.

INDIA

Forum Against Rape, c/o Bombay Women's Centre, 5 Bhavana Apartments, SV Road, Ville Parle West, Bombay 400 056.

The Lawyers Collective, 818, 8th Floor, Stock Exchange Towers, Dalal Street, Bombay-400 023.

Manushi, C1/202 Lajpat Nagar, New Delhi. Tel: 617 022

TRINIDAD AND TOBAGO

Wages for Housework Campaign, c/o Clotil Walcott, Mount Pleasant Road, Arima, Trinidad.

UNITED STATES OF AMERICA

Black Coalition Fighting Back Serial Murders, P.O. Box 3495, Los Angeles, CA 90051. (This is a national address to contact groups in USA cities.)

Congdon & Weed, 298 5th Avenue, New York NY 10001. Tel: 212-736 4883 (Publishers of *Surviving Sexual Assault*. This is a national directory of rape crisis centers, hotlines, and victim assistance programs, with information on prevention and on legal issues.)

Fighting Woman News, P.O. Box 1459, Grand Central Station, New York, NY 10163. (This is a newspaper which lists groups and courses.)

International Wages for Housework Campaign, and International Black Women for Wages for Housework, P.O. Box 3495, Los Angeles, CA 90051. (This is a national address to contact groups in USA cities.)

Legal Action for Women, P.O. Box 14512, San Francisco, CA 94114.

National Center for Prevention and Control of Rape, 200 Independence Avenue, Washington DC. Tel: 301-443 1910 (Publishers of the *National Directory of Rape Prevention and Treatment Resources*.)

National Clearinghouse on Marital Rape, 2325 Oak Street, Berkeley, CA 94708.

National Organization for Victim Assistance, Washington DC.

No Bad Women Just Bad Laws Coalition, P.O. Box 33133, Tulsa, OK 74153.

North American Network of Women Runners, and Women's Fitness Club, P.O. Box 719, Bala Cynwyd, Philadelphia, PA 19004. Tel: 215-668 9886

Revoke Licence to Rape Campaign, P.O. Box 11795, Philadelphia, PA 19101.

Women in Dialogue, P.O. Box 11795, Philadelphia, PA 19101.

Women's Action Alliance, 370 Lexington Avenue, New York, NY 10017. Tel: 212-532 8330 (Publishers of *Women Helping Women. A state-by-state directory of Services*.)

There are very large numbers of self-defence and martial arts clubs right through the USA. Information can be obtained from Mr Jon K. Evans, 11350 Chenault Street, Los Angeles, CA 90049.

(Please note that all information was correct at the time when it was sent to press.)

READING LIST

P. B. Bart and P. H. O'Brien, *Stopping Rape: Successful Survival Strategies* (Pergamon Press, New York and Oxford, 1985)

A. Dickson, *A Woman in Your Own Right: Assertiveness and you* (Quartet Books, London, 1982)

J. Dowdeswell, *Women on Rape* (Thorsons Publishing Group, Wellingborough, 1986)

M. Elliott, *Preventing Child Sexual Assault: A practical guide to talking to children* (Bedford Square Press, London, 1985)

C. Glasman, *True Confessions of a Raspberry* (Centrepiece 4, Housewives in Dialogue, London, 1986)

A. N. Groth, A. W. Burgess, and L. L. Holmstrom, 'Rape, Power, Anger, and Sexuality', *Psychiatry* 134 (1977); reprinted in Ann Wolbert Burgess and Lynda Lytle Holmstrom (eds.), *Rape Crisis and Recovery* (Robert Brady Co., Maryland, 1979)

R. E. Hall, *Ask Any Woman: A London inquiry into rape and sexual assault* (Falling Wall Press, Bristol, 1985)

R. Hall, S. James, and J. Kertész, *The Rapist Who Pays the Rent* (Falling Wall Press, Bristol, 2nd edn. 1984)
This handbook on rape in marriage gives information about how rape laws operate in practice.

Heresies (New York, No. 6, 1978)

W. Hinton, *Fanshen* (Penguin, Harmondsworth, 1972)

S. James (ed.), *Strangers & Sisters: Women, race and immigration* (Falling Wall Press, Bristol, 1985)

M. Kishwar and R. Vanita (eds.), *In Search of Answers: Indian women's voices from Manushi* (Zed Books, London, 1984)

London Rape Crisis Centre, *Sexual Violence: The reality for women* (The Women's Press, London, 1984)

Metropolitan Police Crime Prevention Service, *Positive Steps: Help and advice for women on personal safety* (London, 1986)

R. Norwood, *Women Who Love Too Much* (Arrow Books, London, 1985)

Out From Under (Newsletter of Women Against Abuse, Philadelphia, Winter 1986)

Rape Action Project, *Com.pen.sa.tion* (Boston, 1981). Available from Women In Dialogue, P.O. Box 11795, Philadelphia, PA 19101, USA.

D. E. H. Russell, *Rape in Marriage* (Macmillan, New York, 1982)

C. Walcott, *Fight Back Says a Woman* (Institute of Social Studies, The Hague, 1980)

WinVisible, *Message to Bhopal* (Centrepiece 4, Housewives in Dialogue, London, 1986)

Women Against Rape, *Women at W.A.R.* (Falling Wall Press, Bristol, 1978)
A collection of personal testimonies.

Women In Dialogue, *Every Woman's Handbook on Compensation for Rape and Other Violent Crimes in Pennsylvania* (Philadelphia, 1987). Available from P.O. Box 11795, Philadelphia, PA 19101, USA.

R. Wyre, *Women, Men, and Rape* (Perry Publications, 1986)

ACKNOWLEDGMENTS

The extract on page 19 is taken from *War on Rape* (War on Rape Collective, Melbourne, Australia, 1977).

PICTURE CREDITS
Specially commissioned picture sequences by Norma Harvey (pages 77-112) and Ken Copsey (pages 59-76).
Daily Telegraph 31; Norma Harvey 113, 115, 121; Alvin Hill 120; King's Cross Women's Centre Photo Collective 35 (Lisa Longstaff), 47 (Gigi Turner); London Standard 32; Mail Newspapers PLC 40; Sunday Telegraph 38. Marshall Cavendish would like to thank all those students and friends of the authors who so willingly gave up their time to demonstrate the techniques in the picture sequences.

Drawings by Kevin Maddison.

·INDEX·

Page numbers in italics refer to captions.
Page numbers in bold type show the main entry for a topic.